WHAT
I WISH
I KNEW

Surviving and Thriving
After an Abusive Relationship

A self-empowerment book

by
Dr. Amelia Kelley
and
Kendall Ann Combs

Dedications

First, this book is dedicated to my fellow survivors. I am in awe of your strength. I hope this book provides you with peace and can help you on your journey to healing. This book is truly written for you.

Second, to my Mom. Thank you for teaching me that it's always possible to begin again and there is no such thing as an unsurmountable obstacle or challenge. I am so lucky to have you in my corner. I love you.

Next, this book is dedicated to my father who always reminds me that life is to be lived and enjoyed.

Andrew, thank you for being such a great brother. I appreciate your love and support.

Gretchen, thank you for your unwavering confidence in my dreams and encouraging me to embrace my "sparkle."

Christine, thank you for keeping me laughing through all of our adventures! I am so lucky to have you in my life.

Nina, I cherish our friendship and your honesty and support.

Ozzy and Rocco, my true loves.

Dr. Kelley, the wisdom and honesty you bring to this work is inspiring. Thank you for your insights into my experiences and those of other survivors. This world is a kinder place because of you.

Kendall Ann Combs

The time and energy put into creating this book was paralleled by the time and energy my devoted husband put into running our family, providing me the time to write. He is a true example of a confident man who can stand with and support his partner. To my children, I dedicate this book, so that my daughter always knows what she truly deserves in her relationships, and so that my son is raised with an open and authentic heart.

To my parents, who parented me in such a way as to create the inner narrative: *I can do anything I decide to do.* Without them I would not have the confidence to push myself to do hard things, and they are at the heart of my every success.

To my clients who have opened their hearts and trusted me with their stories: without our relationships I would have learned nothing to put into these pages.

To my dear friend April who reflected on her own past experience with intimate partner violence, I have always been grateful for your love, support and all of the years of laughter.

And finally to Kendall Ann Combs, my co-author, for her bravery and desire to share her story. Without your ability to integrate your past trauma into your present life's mission, this book would not exist.

Dr. Amelia Kelley

Contents

Introduction

"You yourself, as much as anybody in the entire universe deserve your love and affection."
~ Unknown ~

This book is a journey of survival, exploration and service to those who are in, or have been in a relationship wrought with intimidation or control of any kind. If you feel that you have lost a part of yourself, your safety, or what it is you deserve in life, we are here with you. Simply finding this book and cracking open the pages displays an immense level of functioning and self-care, and we hope to offer you everything you came looking for.

The Co-authors, Dr. Amelia Kelley and Kendall Ann Combs, are passionate about helping those who are in abusive relationships achieve safety and peace. Each author will serve to offer her different perspectives, experiences, and expertise to help you manifest your own healing. Additionally, this book can serve as a resource for those in helping professions, or for loved ones supporting someone in an abusive relationship.

Kendall Ann Combs is a survivor of domestic violence who offers help and support to others going through similar situations with her podcast, High Heels and Heartache. She created the podcast to offer advice to survivors and those currently in abusive relationships as a free resource, one she wishes had been available when she was going through her own abuse experience. On her podcast she interviews experts about relationship issues to help her listeners recover from toxic, unhealthy, abusive relationships and to create strong, healthy, long-lasting relationships in all facets of their lives. Much of what she has learned from the various guests on her podcast has inspired the topics covered in this book.

Dr. Amelia Kelley is a licensed therapist with over 15 years of experience and works in her private practice in Cary, North Carolina.

I

Throughout her career she has focused her research and training on serving those recovering from trauma, resulting in attachment and relationship issues. Dr. Kelley came across Kendall Ann's podcast by chance. After reaching out to Kendall Ann they created a powerful episode exploring how trauma impacts the body. Since then the two have continued working together, supporting one another's mission to bring healing to those experiencing abuse and trauma in their relationships.

Just as their meeting was by chance, so too was the idea that generated this book. Both women felt passionate about helping those in abusive relationships, and, as if by fate, the idea of *What I Wish I Knew: Surviving and Thriving After an Abusive Relationship* came to fruition. It is also not by chance that this book came to be during the Me Too Movement, which first began when Tarana Burke, an American social activist and community organizer, started using the phrase "Me Too" as early as 2006. The phrase was later popularized by American actress Alyssa Milano on Twitter in 2017 and has escalated to a poignant stand against sexual assault.

It has been long overdue that there be an increase in awareness about sexual assault as well as other forms of abuse in romantic relationships. This book is critical to this movement as it provides a safe space where a survivor and a licensed professional work together to help guide healing and self-care for those suffering from relationship violence and other forms of abuse.

This book is a place where honest answers will be given, and emotions and experiences will be raw and candid. Some of the book may apply directly to experiences you have had in your own abusive relationship, or perhaps it may be foreshadowing of what could happen if you do not leave before things get worse. There is a saying in the 12 Step Program: "Take what works and leave what doesn't." We encourage you to do the same here. If some of Kendall Ann's story feels unrelatable or some of the recommendations made in the thriving section do not resonate for you, you can take what works for your own personal toolbox and leave the rest. What does not apply now may potentially help in the future or perhaps there may be ideas or skills that someone else in your life may find beneficial.

II

How This Book Works

What you will find in the pages of this book will read part memoir, and part self-empowerment book. We hope Kendall Ann's story will offer synchronicity to some of your own experiences. We know her story is only one example of a survivor's journey; each of you has your own individual story. We designed the layout of this book so you can choose from topics that relate to your own story. Each chapter title states the topic covered in a progressive manner from the beginning stages of an abusive relationship to some of the different forms of abuse that can occur, and finally to leaving and healing from the relationship. Each chapter consists of Kendall Ann's retelling her experience followed by Dr. Kelley providing therapeutic insight about what Kendall Ann went through. Kendall Ann then discusses Dr. Kelley's insights in the "What I Know Now" section of each chapter. There is also a "What Do You Know Now?" page in each chapter so you can record any important conclusions, understanding, or Ah-Ha moments you've had while reading.

If any section in **Part 1** causes distress, we encourage you to practice self-care by skipping that section and reading the following chapter or you can choose to move on to read **Part 2.** This subsequent section will offer helpful support and information about thriving after abuse no matter where you are in your own story.

For professionals or emotional support persons:

We would encourage you to read the book in its entirety. If you are supporting or serving someone who is sharing their abuse story, that person may or may not be able to share all of it. There are many possible reasons for this: fear, trauma response, dissociation or repression of feelings, or difficulty trusting others. Reading Kendall Ann's entire story offers a broad example of what someone experiencing abuse might endure.

To the survivors who are reading this book for counsel and support: You can reach out, connect, and find resources through our author's

III

pages at; www.ameliakelley.com and www.kendallanncombs.com. You can use these sites to contact the authors for further information or for any questions that arise while reading the book.

Within the pages of this book you will find writing prompts, exercises, as well as the "What Do You Know Now" section at the end of every chapter. This section is intended for you to express your thoughts, feelings and reflections on what you learned in that chapter. We have left the page blank, without lines, in the case that you would like to express yourself using; art, poetry, collaging or any other form of expression you desire. If you do not feel safe documenting anything in the book, feel free to write in a separate journal. One safe option is to use an online, password protected journaling website for completing the exercises from the book. Alternatively, you can choose to skip writing altogether and simply read and reflect on the questions and exercises.

In addition to Kendall Ann's story of survival, this book provides research-supported interventions, coping skills, and methods to seek safety. You will receive psychoeducation focusing on how to thrive and connect with yourself again as you work through the emotional pain that results from abuse. You will learn about the different phases of abuse as well as gain a greater understanding of risk factors, warning signs, and specific ways to cope with these issues. You will learn how to get out safely, the potential risks related to trauma response, and finally how to thrive and heal once you are free from the relationship. Most importantly we want this book, the podcast High Heels and Heartache and the resources offered, to help you feel supported. We are here to help.

Part 1: Surviving

Chapter 1

The Fairytale Relationship

*"The devil doesn't come dressed in a red cape and pointy horns.
He comes as everything you've ever wished for."*
~ Tucker Max ~

It was years in the making but this was the moment of truth: I was lying on my back on the cold, linoleum floor while a man twice my size suffocated and strangled me, banging my head against the floor beneath me. I fought to breathe, my vision began to blur, my ears rang, and my head ached. This was the moment when I either became a woman killed by her intimate partner, or a woman who survived. Either way, I would come to understand that what I didn't know could hurt me, and quite possibly even kill me.

My only education about domestic violence was from Lifetime Movies, specifically *Mother May I Sleep With Danger (1996)*. In that movie, a virtuous Tori Spelling is nearly murdered by her wrong side of the tracks, elusively dangerous boyfriend. It led me to believe that the early warning signs of an abuser would be easy to spot. I imagined in the beginning of the relationship an abuser would have a heart of gold, but a bad temper. He'd probably be riding a motorcycle and would be mean to waiters. These were the signs I thought I should be looking for.

Before my abusive relationship, one myth I believed was that abuse didn't happen to women like me. I was a successful, young professional with a Master's degree. I had no problem standing up for myself against anyone who tried to control me. I was financially stable, mature, and determined not to waste my time in relationships that I didn't think would be long- lasting matches. Although I had recently moved to a city

1

where I knew no one, I still had a strong network of friends and a close family with whom I spoke to daily. I spent my evenings at dance class trying to keep up with the younger members, laughing about how something that once came so easily to me now required more thought and practice than ever before. I loved nothing more than spending time with my dog, Ozzy, hiking new trails or cuddling with him at home. I was smart, strong and independent. I would never be anyone's victim. I couldn't have been more wrong.

The Fairy Tale Begins

I met him online. Although I had been taking a break from dating to concentrate on my career, I promised my mom I'd go on one date a month. He and I exchanged a few brief texts before we decided to meet. On the evening of the date I begrudgingly applied minimal makeup and slipped on my green "first date" dress: a short, plunging sheath that made the heat of August in the South more bearable. I promised myself I'd stay the whole meal before using the "I have to let my dog out" excuse. Unaware of what lay ahead of me, I drove to the restaurant.

Upon my arrival I instantly recognized him from his pictures, and although he was shorter than he had indicated in his profile, I thought he was handsome, and I regretted not putting more energy into my own appearance. We spent the evening eating pizza, drinking wine, and laughing. It was the best first date I had ever had and before I knew it, the bartender was kicking us out. My date walked me to my car, and we shared a passionate kiss before he asked if he could see me later that week. I quickly agreed and drove away finally believing the saying, "When you know, you know." I thought I had found *the one*.

Our courtship started the next day when I awoke to texts saying, "Good morning, Beautiful" and "How do I miss you already?" I was relieved I wasn't the only one who had sensed the magic between us. On our second date I did most of the talking. He was surprisingly interested in my life, my goals, my past, and what I wanted in a relationship. I was flattered at how curious he was about my life. It was a refreshing change from previous dates I had gone on with men where I mostly nodded and smiled barely saying a word. When I asked him questions about himself, he would tell me that he'd rather talk about me. It made me blush and a warm sensation covered my body.

For our third date we went to his parents' house to swim in their pool. I was surprised to see his parents were home. I had not anticipated meeting them so early in the relationship, and I instantly became nervous. His father and stepmother were warm and welcoming, but I was caught off guard when his father began commenting on things he had seen on my online professional profile. He congratulated me for the awards I had won and asked a lot of questions about my job. It seemed odd, and something in my gut alerted me that this was strange, but his father's easy-going style of conversation disarmed me. When we were alone, I asked my date why he didn't tell me that his parents were going to be home. He told me he didn't know they'd be there, but I sensed he was lying. He told me it wasn't a big deal because he could tell they loved me and listed all the reasons why. Flattered, I let the lie slide since I had no proof, and we enjoyed the rest of the day at the pool.

Within a month, I was spending most of my free time with him. Sometimes I even chose to spend time with him instead of going to the dance classes I loved so much. On our date nights, I greeted him by jumping into his arms and he'd spin me around. We called it our "Bachelor Show Greeting." It felt like a dream. I congratulated myself for not settling for any of the men I had dated before and for holding out for someone so perfect.

Each night was filled with profound conversations. I told him all of my deepest fears. How I was scared to have a marriage end in divorce. How I felt like I was never really understood by those around me. How lonely it was to move to a city where I had no friends. How I longed to feel a deep connection to someone who would love and support me without fail. He held my hands and listened intently. He expressed how his father's battle with cancer scared him and how he was happy to finally have someone to talk to about it. I was flattered he trusted me enough to be so vulnerable.

One day when we visited his parents at their lake house, he convinced me that I should try water skiing for the first time. He enthusiastically jumped off the boat with me. As we treaded water, tow rope in my hands, I confessed how terrified I was to fail in front of him and his parents. He looked deeply into my eyes and told me he knew I could do it. It filled my heart with love. I finally had someone who believed in me unconditionally, who trusted I could do anything, even when I was unsure. Even when my attempt to ski failed, he expressed how proud he was that I tried and how brave I was. We shared a passionate kiss and he told me that he loved me and I, of course, said the same. It felt like a fairytale.

I fell for him fast and hard. He was everything I had ever wanted: handsome, educated, kind, and caring. It was a dream. I had never felt so strongly about anyone before. I relished the time I spent with him, hanging on every word he said, and every minute we spent apart I was desperate to reunite with him. The nights when we didn't have plans to see each other we'd end up texting or talking on the phone throughout the evening and into the early morning. On many of those nights the magnetism between us was so strong that one of us would end up jumping into their car, pajama-clad, to sleep next to the other. We couldn't stand to be apart.

"Kendall Ann," he said one day as we walked our dogs, hand in hand, "you are the most wonderful person in the world, and I am so happy I didn't settle for someone else that I didn't love as much as I love you." This became a theme of our conversations: how lucky we were to have each other and the debt we owed to the universe for bringing us together. Two people who were so perfect for each other. So happy. So fortunate.

He planned romantic dates based solely on the things I liked. We went to my favorite restaurants, saw the movies I was curious about in theaters, and of course took our dogs on long hikes complete with romantic picnics of my favorite foods and sometimes even a bottle of champagne.

As an outside salesperson, many of my days were filled with driving all over the state to meet with potential clients. Countless times I'd return home to beautiful bouquets of flowers from him waiting for my return outside of my apartment. Other nights when I was shackled to my computer preparing quotes or presentations for the next day, he'd have my favorite pizza delivered so I wouldn't have to take the time to cook.

Everything he did was thoughtful and sweet. One evening he invited me over for wine by the firepit at his house and when I arrived he handed me my favorite wine in a glass with my name on it.

"What's this?" I asked. "Is my name on this glass?"

"I wanted a reminder of the most beautiful words I have ever heard to always be here, even when you're not," he said sweetly.

Butterflies filled my stomach. We made s'mores and talked about our future all night, kissing passionately, laughing, and slow dancing under the stars. It felt like magic.

Our chemistry and care for each other was evident in our sexual relationship. Sometimes sweet, sometimes playful but always satisfying. As my love for him deepened, my sexual desire for him grew. I finally had a man that could satisfy every need I had, mind, body, and soul.

Soon he was planning trips for us to visit cities to watch my favorite NFL team play and he promised me that together we'd accomplish my goal of seeing my favorite team, the Detroit Lions, play in every NFL stadium. He made all of the arrangements, bought the tickets to the games, and researched the best places to go in the cities. My only responsibility was to pick the city and he happily did the rest. The trips were exciting and fun: ghost tours and swamp tours in New Orleans. Listening to country music in dive bars in Nashville. During those trips he was the perfect companion. He was sensitive to my fear about missing flights and showed no frustration at my need to arrive at the airport hours early. As we walked through the airport he carried my bags and, on the plane, he insisted on sitting in the middle seat so I could have more room in the aisle seat.

I couldn't help but brag to my family and friends about my perfect boyfriend and the message from them all was the same, "You deserve it." They were thrilled that I had found my happy ending. My person. My dream man. I finally had the love I had craved for so long. All of the broken relationships, the bad first dates, the tears I shed over other men who had treated me poorly were worth it because they led me to this wonderful man who was so thoughtful, so kind, so devoted to my happiness.

The relationship transformed me. His love, devotion and faith in me gave me a confidence I never had before. He accepted and loved all parts of me, even the ones that I struggled to accept, or other men had wanted to change. One winter we traveled to Florida to escape the cold. As we walked on the beach with our dogs I dared him to jump into the ocean. He laughed as he refused and challenged me to do it instead. Never the one to say "no" to a dare, I changed into my bathing suit and plunged into the frigid water later that afternoon. When I ran out of the water he was waiting on the shore, cozy blanket extended in his arms to warm me.

He wrapped the blanket around me, and we laughed with such thunder at the ridiculousness of my swim that we fell to the ground. As we lay there, his arms around me, he whispered how he loved this part of me. My joy. My love of life. And that he could never be happy without me. It was one of the only times in my life that I felt seen. I knew in my heart that he was my soulmate and that he and I would share a thousand moments like this together. As we lay there, we both cried tears of joy, of belonging, and of love. It was the most connected I ever felt to another person.

I was one of the lucky ones. I had found true love.

What Is Love Bombing?

The early romance of Kendall Ann and her date can be relatable for anyone who has searched for love and experienced the feelings of a new and exciting relationship. Finding your match, or someone who cares deeply for you, is important to most people at some stage in their lives. As humans we are social beings and by nature, we are designed to need people for survival, meaning and joy. This is not to say that all people need the same number of social relationships and connections, but at least a few meaningful relationships are essential for mental health and wellness. This need for connection is supported by science. Research shows that meaningful interactions with others, where there is safety and quality in the relationship, has protective factors against aging and can improve immune health. Even at a basic biological level, we are innately drawn to connection.

When first meeting someone, we hope we can trust our instincts about whether that person will be a positive influence on our lives. When someone works at making us feel special or wanted, we hope and often expect that these gestures are coming from a genuine and safe space, and often times it is. The idea of *"love at first sight"* is not completely impossible; some relationships really do click and get off to a fast start. However, there are two key elements to this kind of experience that differ from love bombing.

Mutuality: Fast-paced courtships that are not an example of love bombing are mutual in nature, meaning both people feel completely comfortable with the pace of the relationship.

Pace: The pace of the relationship leaves each person with positive feelings, as they each sustain their individual identities, and there is little to no imbalance of power.

An example where pace was an issue in Kendall Ann's relationship was on the third date. Her date was speeding up the pace of the relationship by introducing her to his parents without checking in with her first. For some, meeting a love interest's parents can be nerve-wracking and is a big deal, and if he were respecting her pacing of the relationship, he would have asked her if she was ready to meet them.

Love bombing, which is a weapon many predators (or narcissists) employ at the beginning of a relationship, is hard to detect. It can mask itself as a fast-paced, love at first sight type of relationship. The difficulty in detecting love bombing lies in the fact that it feels good at first, until *eventually it doesn't*. Simply put, it is an attempt to influence or manipulate a person by demonstrations of attention and affection. It can be displayed in various ways, and often results in an unequal division of power and control in the long-term outcomes of a relationship. Love bombing offers tidbits of love that can result in learned helplessness, or yearning for more, when the relationship later becomes unhealthy.

Why Love Bombing Works and Why It Is Dangerous

The positive feelings that love bombing elicits are potent and effective. These feelings can be intoxicating and make it hard to focus on much else other than the love bomber. Being told how important or special you are feels wonderful; luckily not everyone who expresses love and adoration is trying to hurt or control you. Love bombing is also coupled with manipulative efforts to retain control of most aspects of the relationship. These efforts are so gradual, they are often hard to detect unless you are looking for them.

The master goal of love bombing is to **manipulate focus and attention onto the love bomber**. The motivation for doing so can be attributed to the need for power, control, and idolization of a narcissist. It can also be a dangerous result of a predator working to groom their victim by making them feel safe when they are with the love bomber. Consequently, when things start to take a turn for the worse, the point of reference is skewed, and the victim is more likely to believe that there is always a way back to *the way things once were.*

One other way a love bomber tries to gain control is through purposeful information gathering, which was seen on Kendall Ann's earlier dates with her abuser. The love bomber can use your own insecurities, hopes, dreams, and failings against you. The more they *learn and know* about you, the more they can use against you. You can decipher between genuine interest and purposeful information gathering when the love bomber is hesitant to disclose their own personal information. When things go badly, the love bomber will remind you of "how good you are together" or may focus on what matters most to you. This can include things they may have learned during the information gathering stage or things that make you feel most insecure if you were to leave the relationship. These tactics are also a method of control found in the **repair stages** in an abusive relationship, right after a serious fight or threats of safety occurs. We will learn more about these stages in Chapter 3, *Power of Control*.

Putting it simply, love bombing can create a level of trust in someone who should not be trusted. It can make you question yourself, leading to being more agreeable with requests made by the love bomber, such as cutting out relationships because your love bomber does not like someone who is important to you in your life. Their reasons for exclusion can vary, but often their objective lies in removing someone they see as a threat to your enmeshed relationship. The reasons for why abusers limit your social sphere and try to establish power will be explored further as Kendall Ann's story unfolds.

One thing is clear, it can be difficult to identify when someone is love bombing, especially at the beginning of a relationship. That is why awareness of what love bombing is and carefully listening to your intuition and internal reactions are crucial.

Love Bombing And Kendall Ann's Story

At the beginning of Kendall Ann's story there was a point where her tone shifted slightly from elation and attraction to slight trepidation. As mentioned previously, this happened when she was introduced to her date's family at a very early stage and without any warning. His father's awareness of her life and details about who she was before she even met him made her uncomfortable. She had not been given the chance to share details about who she was in in her own time, instead her date had taken charge.

These moments of discomfort are indicators that the relationship was not entirely healthy. *Something was off.* We will explore many of these types of moments in this book which we will refer to as **Red Flags**. Together we will map out these particular warning signs that can occur at

Together we will map out these particular warning signs that can occur at different stages of a relationship. By doing so you can become mindful of them, as awareness and knowledge both increase safety. You can find a list of these warning signs at the end of the book.

What I Now Know

1. Love bombing is a drug, and your partner is the dealer.

Texts, flowers, kind words, and extraordinary commitment can be intoxicating. These acts flooded my brain with the hormones and chemicals that gave me a natural high. I had no idea how far I'd fall when the high passed, and I had no idea the lengths I'd go to feel that high again. Now I realize my abuser did all of those things to hook me and to make me feel connected to him. The more interested he was in me and my life, the closer I felt to him. The level of intensity in our relationship did not match the time that had been invested. We were moving very fast, very soon. It felt like a love story out of a movie. I know now that no matter what concessions I made, or what parts of myself I abandoned, he'd never again be the man from the first months of our relationship, because that was not the real him.

2. *"Do not tell secrets to those whose faith and silence has not already been tested."* ~ *Queen Elizabeth* ~

I remember reading this when I was young and thinking it was truly sage advice. I wish I would have remembered the quotation during the early stages of my relationship. By sharing my most intimate thoughts, fears, and desires so early, I basically gave him all the information he needed to become the person I wanted and needed. I was telling him these secrets because I was desperate to be heard and understood and I was thankful to have found someone who cared about my feelings – finally. I had no clue the information would be used to manipulate me. I held the private information he disclosed to me as sacred, but I see now how these little scraps were only revealed to give me a sense that we were both sharing what was most sacred to us.

3. Your gut is almost never wrong. Listen to it.

I know now that I need to listen to my gut instinct when something feels wrong in a relationship. I was so nervous about creating problems and possibly losing my relationship that I wasn't acting on my gut instincts when I felt my abuser was lying or trying to manipulate me. Had I been paying attention to my instincts I would have focused more on protecting myself. Going forward, when I notice my gut talking, I listen even if it means I need to assert myself and possibly be rejected. My abuser was lying about not knowing his parents would be home when he took me to their house and although I couldn't prove it, I knew it in my heart. There were other small lies I chose to ignore during the love bombing stage because everything else was so wonderful. This was a huge mistake. Now I know I don't want to have a relationship with anyone who lies ever again.

What Do You Know Now?

*This section is intended for you to convey your thoughts,
feelings and reflections on what you learned in the chapter by writing
or using other creative forms of expression.*

Chapter 2

Emotional Abuse

"All this time I drank you like the cure when maybe you were the poison."
~ *Clementine Von Radics* ~

On one of our earliest dates we hiked with our dogs through the State Park near my date's house. I was elated when our dogs met and instantly liked each other. *This is going to be perfect*, I thought. It was not perfect. After only ten minutes of hiking in the summer heat, his dog decided he had enough and laid down. I couldn't blame him. I had already sweat through most of my clothes and was nearly finished with the bottle of water I was holding. We decided to retreat to his house and watch a movie in the air conditioning.

When we got to his house, I asked to use the bathroom to freshen up. As I walked down the hallway I was shocked to see three, framed picture collages of my date with a thin, blonde woman. My stomach lurched as I realized the pictures had to be of his ex. Why did he still have pictures of his ex-girlfriend hanging in his home if they had broken up months ago? Had he lied about the timeline of their breakup on our first date? Fearing it would ruin what was left of our date, I tried to convince myself not to bring it up. Despite my best efforts, I just couldn't hold it in.

Entering the living room where he was sitting on the sofa I asked, "Why do you have pictures of your ex all over the hallway if you broke up with her months ago?"

He laughed and reached for my hand, pulling me onto his lap.

15

"I cannot believe that the most beautiful woman on the planet would be so insecure about a couple of pictures," he said stroking my hair. "I thought you'd have way more confidence than that! You're so jealous!"

"I'm not jealous!" I protested.

I wanted to tell him it didn't make me feel insecure or jealous. It made me think he had lied about the timeline of his previous relationship, but I didn't speak up. He started to laugh and tickle me, distracting me from the anxiety I had about the pictures.

A week later when I was at his home again, I was shocked to see the pictures still hung on the wall. "Dude," I said curtly, "take those pictures down. For real."

Again, he laughed. "Uh oh! There's my jealous girlfriend again!"

It angered me this time. "I'm not jealous. It's disrespectful that you're inviting me to your home and keeping pictures of your ex displayed."

He shrugged. "Okay, okay. Who knew you were sensitive about stupid things like this?"

I was torn. *Was I being overly sensitive? Was it not as big of a deal as I thought it was? Shouldn't my boyfriend be trying to protect me from pain rather than leaving pictures displayed that he knew made me feel uncomfortable?*

I decided to put it out of my mind.

The next week he made me dinner at his home. After dinner, I went to the bathroom before we moved into the living room to watch a movie. The damn pictures were *still* hanging in the hallway. Filled with courage from the three glasses of wine I drank during dinner, I removed the frames from the wall and quietly deposited them into the kitchen trashcan without telling him. I couldn't shake the awful feeling that he had left them up to taunt me in some way, to remind me there were others before me who found him desirable or who would be willing to take my place if I didn't behave properly.

They are just pictures, I thought. I gathered my composure and walked into the living room. *Don't make a mountain out of a molehill. Those pictures mean nothing to him, which is probably why they are still up. If he thought about them, he'd already have taken them down.*

Part of me knew I was trying to convince myself of something

16

that was not true. Instead of confronting him about my feelings, I chose to ignore them. I wasn't going to ruin my relationship with a perfect man over some stupid pictures of his ex.

In my early 20s I began smoking cigarettes. I didn't consider myself a smoker, but many times I smoked when I was feeling stressed or when I drank alcohol. This was something I was working on changing and I had made it clear on my dating profile that I didn't want to date someone who smoked. We had discussed this on our first date, and he confided that he had just quit smoking, so we would be able to hold each other accountable for being cigarette free. One night when he came to pick me up I tasted cigarettes when he kissed me.

"Have you been smoking?" I asked.

"No!" he answered stepping backward away from me.

"I can taste it on you," I said.

"Why would I lie about that?" he replied.

I stood in the breezeway of my apartment building perplexed. *Why would he lie about that?* I was puzzled. I knew I tasted cigarettes, but he also denied smoking. I decided that maybe he just had a slip up and was embarrassed to admit it. Like everyone else, I had sometimes lied when my behavior wasn't perfect so I could empathize. I let it slide.

The next time he picked me up for a date he again tasted like cigarettes.

"Just be honest with me," I said, "are you smoking?"

"I can't be with you if you keep accusing me of something every time I pick you up," he said defensively.

With that he turned and walked out of my apartment. I stood in place thinking he just needed a minute and would come right back. When he didn't return after fifteen minutes I went to look in the parking lot. His car was gone. He had left.

Panic set in. I had ruined it. I had pushed too hard, and it was over. I texted and called several times that night with no response. When I woke up the next morning I checked my phone immediately. Nothing. I called and texted again. No answer.

Later that afternoon there was a knock at the door. I was surprised to see a deliveryman with a huge bouquet. They were from my boyfriend. The note simply said, "I'm sorry."

17

I placed the bouquet on my dining room table and sat staring at it. *Why is he sending me flowers if he's not texting me back? What exactly is he saying he's sorry for?*

I dialed his number and he finally answered. He offered no explanation for not answering for almost a whole day. Instead he confessed that he was still smoking but was going to try harder to quit and he needed my help to do it. It struck me as odd that he never apologized for lying but I didn't want to push him away or abandon him since he said he needed my help. I chose to forgive him and move on. Within two weeks I was smoking cigarettes.

Lying about smoking wasn't his only perplexing behavior. One evening, we made plans for me to come to his house so he could make me dinner. When I arrived, he was sitting at the kitchen table, scissors in hand, cutting a recipe out of a magazine.

"Come give me a kiss," he shouted enthusiastically when I walked in the back door.

I bounded over and gave him a huge kiss. He pulled me onto his lap.

"Be careful with those scissors!" I joked.

"Look at how good these recipes look," he said spinning me around, so I was still on his lap but now facing away from him.

"They do look good," I agreed, slowly flipping the pages of the magazine. "Look how delicious this cake looks," I said pointing to a picture of a three-layer carrot cake.

He didn't answer.

I looked over my shoulder. He was staring at me, a severed lock of my hair in one hand, scissors in the other.

I jumped from his lap. "Did you just cut my hair?" I screamed.

"No! I don't know what happened! I was just sitting here with the scissors in my hand, and I must have accidentally cut your hair while I was looking over your shoulder at the magazine. Oh my god, Kendall Ann, I am so sorry. I promise, I'd never do something like that to you! Why would I ever do that?" He said walking toward me.

He hugged me tightly. "Please believe me. It was an accident."

I said nothing. We stood in the kitchen for several minutes, hugging in silence.

How did he accidentally cut my hair? He's lying. Wait. What

18

kind of person would purposely cut my hair and lie about it. It's so weird. It had to be an accident.

"You believe me. Right, Kendall Ann?" he asked, looking pathetic.

Mostly, I did believe him because the only other explanation was that this man just cut my hair for no reason and then lied.

Cautiously, I nodded.

"Thank God!" he whispered taking my hands in his. "I will never ever hurt you," he said looking into my eyes. "I love you and I promise I will protect you against anyone or anything that tries to hurt you."

It was what I wanted to hear my whole life. I had found my partner and I wasn't alone. I pushed the haircutting from my mind and tried to enjoy the rest of the evening.

Our relationship continued to move quickly. Within three months I was living in the house he rented from his stepmother, and we were searching for a house to buy together. I still had several months left on the lease of my apartment and told him I would end the lease early. I went so far as to write a letter to the leasing office and told my family and friends I was terminating my lease, but I never took the letter to the leasing office. Each time I tried, I backed out and I didn't have the ability to express why. There was some part of me telling me to keep my place.

As the months rolled by, I started to lose myself. Things that I held as truths were constantly being questioned by him. He seemed to be an expert on anything I thought I was knowledgeable about. He would explain that he was trying to make me better. Certainly, he didn't want me to embarrass myself and say stupid things to other people that he knew were wrong, but how did he know so much about everything?

I was also losing connections to the things I loved. Each Tuesday when I returned from dance class, he would tell me how much he and the dogs missed me and would question how it was so easy for me to leave all of them. "I guess you just don't love me as much as I love you," he'd say and walk away.

After several Tuesdays of the same conversation, I stopped going to dance class all together. Instead I joined the gym he attended and centered my workout times around his schedule. *He just loves me so much that he can't stand to be away from me,* I told myself. I felt happy that I had found someone so devoted to me, but each Tuesday I woke up with a sense of yearning for the dance class I wouldn't be attending.

By the time our relationship hit the eight-month mark, it looked very different from the way it began. My mood began to depend solely upon his. On his happy days, things were as they had been in the beginning, filled with laughter and fun, kindness and care. But on other days, a dark cloud settled over the house and I very quickly learned I needed to act accordingly. Suddenly, I was responsible for elevating my boyfriend's mood. I felt responsible for his happiness even if I was not the one who had caused whatever was bothering him. I walked on eggshells and hoped not to displease him in any way.

Most days I found that if I simply agreed with whatever he wanted or said, the tension would slowly melt and by the time I went to sleep in the evening, the knot in my stomach would begin to untie. Sometimes I felt my mere presence was an annoyance to him. I began to feel I needed to justify my place in the relationship all the time. I wanted him to see that I was still the person he had loved so passionately only a few months earlier.

When the bad days began to pile on top of each other and the pressure was too much for me to take, he would suddenly readjust his mood and be the light-hearted man I had fallen for. But even on those "good" days, I dared not do anything to make the dark part of him reappear. As with any couple there were arguments, but they never seemed to reach any resolution. I found myself taking blame more often than not for being "too sensitive" or "overreacting" in an effort to keep the peace. Many arguments were simply never resolved and never spoken of again. Some nights we'd spend the whole evening bickering, we'd go to bed angry and the next day he would not acknowledge there even had been an argument. This caused great confusion in me. Only hours before he had been so passionate about his opinion and perspectives, then they would evaporate by the next morning. It made it difficult to know what was actually important to him and what wasn't. I struggled to decide whether or not to address our previous difference of opinion.

One constant source of friction was around his driving. In my teenage years I had been a passenger in a car accident, causing me to be fearful in the car even years later. Despite my sharing this with him, he remained an aggressive driver. Riding in the car with him was very uncomfortable.

Sometimes, I'd get the courage to tell him that his driving scared me. He always said I needed to "get over it." When I would offer to drive he would never let me. Instead, he'd speed down the road as I clutched the car door. He made me feel guilty for being afraid. He complained that my criticism of his driving was hurtful. His words often led me to be the one to apologize for emotionally wounding him even though I was the one in fear. At night I would lie in bed thinking about how many things I had changed to please him, while he showed an unwillingness to make even the smallest compromises. Then miraculously we'd have a really good day, and I'd forget the sleepless night before. Without realizing it I had slowly surrendered my right to decide what kind of day I wanted to have. Instead, he decided for me.

My confusion about the sleepless nights and manipulation of my feelings sprang from loving him deeply – despite everything. He was still the man that held me in his arms on the beach as we shared tears of joy at how happy our connection made us feel. Many times, he still showed me endless love and was devoted to my every need. He would perform huge acts of kindness to prove I was still the most important part of his life. At times I found myself driving miles on the highway lost in thought about how to fix the uncertainty I felt about our relationship. My thoughts would distract me from what I was doing or where I was going.

He was so unpredictable. Sometimes he'd charge into the house after work and collapse into my arms with overwhelming vulnerability. "Please don't leave me. I know I'm not perfect. I'll be better. I promise, I'll be better," he'd confess, his warm tears on my shoulder. We'd sit there together, tangled up with each other and my confusion would lift. He was still my soulmate. My partner. My love.

One night we were having wine at the bar of one our favorite restaurants, and we began discussing a possible career change for me.

"You'll have no problem," he remarked "because you have two degrees. Not like me."

"Do you want to go get a master's?" I asked. "What do you think you'd want to study?"

He chuckled, "First I'd need a bachelor's to get a master's!"

21

It was a gut punch.

"I'm confused. I thought you had your bachelor's," I said trying to make sense of this contradictory information.

"I don't," he replied with a shrug. "Is that a problem?"

I had to think for a moment. I didn't care that he didn't have his degree, but I cared deeply about his lying about having one.

"It's a problem because you lied."

"I should have told you," he said looking down at his wine glass. "I was just intimidated because you have two degrees!"

"But you didn't know I had two degrees when you filled out your dating profile," I said feeling my face redden with frustration.

He slammed his wine glass onto the bar, shattering it. I jumped off my stool in fear.

"You're acting like I am a liar. I am not a liar. You didn't ask me if I ever finished college, so I didn't lie. You're such a snob. You really think you're better than me because you have more education but I'm much smarter than you," he sneered, sticking his finger into my face.

He turned and walked out of the restaurant leaving me standing at the bar, broken glass and wine in front of me. The bartender looked at me with concern.

"Can I please pay for these?" My voice shook as I asked him. I paid the tab and walked out under a cloud of embarrassment. I found my boyfriend sitting in his car in the parking lot.

"I'm sorry," he said through tears as I buckled my seatbelt. "Please don't break up with me because I didn't finish college."

"You're missing the point. I don't care whether or not you graduated from college; it's the lie that is upsetting me. No more lies. Promise?" I reached over and wiped a tear from his cheek.

"I'm so lucky," he replied. He grabbed my hand and gently raised it to his lips and kissed it.

For days, the lie hung heavy upon me. *Was this an isolated incident or was this the first of many deceptions that I'll uncover? How many times have I foolishly believed his lies? Surely this is the only fabrication, right? This is true love and there's no room for deceit in true love. Am I overreacting?*

Confused, I made a plan. Moving forward I wouldn't blindly trust everything he said. I'd dig. I'd look for evidence. Then, once I knew he wasn't a liar I could go back to trusting what he said and not need proof. Over time I found that constantly having to double check and confirm everything he said was exhausting and impossible to maintain, so I went back to trusting him, but still there was an unease in me.

I lived in a state of constant confusion. Yes, he's a liar. No, he's not. Yes, he loves me deeply and wants us to be happy. No, he only cares for himself and not me. I kept wishing we could go back to the days when kindness and laughter filled the majority of our relationship, not consternation and agitation. This man was sometimes the exact same person I'd fallen in love with and other times a stranger I didn't know.

On one of his darker mornings, he complained that the refrigerator wasn't smelling fresh. As soon as he walked out of the door, I immediately snapped into action and began cleaning it from top to bottom. I read the expiration date of everything and discarded anything even close to smelling old. I poured the contents of a Rubbermaid bowl down the sink and turned on the disposal. It ground to a stop.

Shit. I thought. *This is going to get really bad.* I called an emergency plumber who promised me he'd have it fixed by the time my boyfriend came home from work that day. The plan didn't work. My boyfriend arrived home to the plumber removing the contents of the bowl from the pipes with his hands and explaining that I had put too much down the drain for the pipes to handle. My boyfriend laughed loudly.

"You'd think someone with a master's degree would be a little smarter than that!" The plumber looked at me with concern. I could tell he was embarrassed for me. I said nothing. Once the disposal was fixed, I paid the plumber and he left.

When we were alone again, my boyfriend turned to me, disgusted, "You're a fucking moron," he hissed.

"I was trying to do something nice by cleaning out the fridge and I made a mistake. I paid for the mistake to be fixed and I'd prefer not to talk about it anymore." I defended myself.

"Okay," he said, "you fucking moron."

I slept on the couch that night, and you know what, I felt like a moron.

23

The Cycle of Abuse

As Kendall Ann's relationship started to show more warning signs of abuse, it is important to be aware of the Cycle of Abuse that is present in most abusive relationships. The Cycle of Abuse describes the ongoing, cyclical pattern most abusive relationships follow. We encourage you to review this cycle to increase your awareness so you can reflect on your own relationship from an objective perspective. The image below shows each stage of the potentially endless cycle of abuse, all of which will be explored in subsequent chapters.

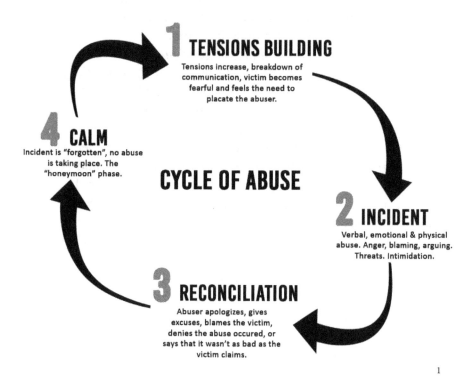

1 TENSIONS BUILDING

Tensions increase, breakdown of communication, victim becomes fearful and feels the need to placate the abuser.

4 CALM

Incident is "forgotten", no abuse is taking place. The "honeymoon" phase.

CYCLE OF ABUSE

2 INCIDENT

Verbal, emotional & physical abuse. Anger, blaming, arguing. Threats. Intimidation.

3 RECONCILIATION

Abuser apologizes, gives excuses, blames the victim, denies the abuse occured, or says that it wasn't as bad as the victim claims.

1

---

1   The cycle of abuse is a social cycle theory developed in 1979 by Lenore E. Walker to explain patterns of behavior in an abusive relationship.

Tensions Building

The Tensions Building stage of Kendall Ann's relationship is evident in the way that *love bombing* progressed things forward from casual dating to a serious relationship in what she described as a short amount of time. After only three months, the two were living together. For some, such a time frame makes sense, but for many, it is incredibly fast. The *honeymoon phase* of their relationship, when most people are riding the high feel-good love hormones and idealized versions of their partner, was already riddled with conflict and attempts by her abuser to reduce Kendall Ann's self-esteem. Between his insecure comments made about her education, degrading her in public in front of the bartender at the restaurant and then later the plumber in their home, her abuser had one main goal – to reduce her self-esteem to a state lower than his own. By doing this he could better control and manipulate her, which is just one part of a never-ending cycle when emotional abuse is used as a weapon.

In the Tensions Building portion of the Cycle of Abuse a victim often feels the need to placate their abuser. Kenall Ann began agreeing with nearly everything her abuser said in order to prevent conflict. She took blame for arguments that she did not initiate and felt responsible for his happiness even if she was not at fault. Her abuser's unpredictable behavior also served to further build the tension in their relationship. Kendall Ann began to be fearful of his mood and how it would afect their interactions. Another way that her abuser manipulated her during this stage was through a technique called *gaslighting*.

What Is Gaslighting?

Almost anyone can fall victim to gaslighting because the ploy can be very effective. *Gaslighting* is an attempt to instill doubt in one's own perception of reality, mainly the reality based on your own persona, ego strengths, and values. This tactic is often carried out by narcissists, psychopaths, or abusers, as well as dictators or cult leaders. It is hard to detect, as the techniques of gaslighting are instituted slowly and increase in intensity over time. Here we have a **Red Flag** – one that can be very

25

difficult to spot because of the confusion it generates.

A common theme of gaslighting is **deception**. There are various ways in which an abuser can use deception and lying as forms of gaslighting. One way is with blatant denial of personal wrongdoing by the abuser. This type of deception was very present in Kendall Ann's relationship when her abuser cut her hair without her permission and then denied it. He manipulated the truth, trying to make Kendall Ann think she was crazy for thinking he would do such a thing intentionally. Kendall Ann mentioned how bizarre the situation appeared, questioning her own experience. Kendall Ann talked about being confused on more than one occasion, which is exactly what gaslighting does. It distorts reality just enough to create uncertainty in your own thoughts and opinions.

Another form of deception found in gaslighting is **indirect persuasion**. This form of gaslighting occurs after the stages of love-bombing where you have grown to idealize your abuser. Once they have your trust, they can more effectively make suggestions that are not conducive to your actual desires, appearing innocent while doing so. Jackson MacKenzie outlines this tactic in his book, *Psychopath Free*, where the gaslighter insults someone from a past relationship, while complimenting you in order to get you to comply with things they want from you.

Here are some examples given in this book:

My ex and I always fought	We never fight
My ex always needed to talk on the phone	You're not needy or demanding
My ex would always nag me about getting a job	You're so much more understanding

These "compliments" are effective forms of manipulation and efforts to silence your desires, needs, and emotions. If you choose to express contrasting thoughts, your abuser will likely counter with the silent treatment or other forms of verbal aggression whether it be blatant or passive aggressive. Having your own opinion puts you at risk of losing the idealized version of you they created. Kendall Ann mentioned she felt she had to "walk on eggshells," and keep her own views and opinions to herself or run the risk of her abuser slipping into one of his bad moods, which he would take out on her. Feeling like you need to censor yourself constantly or "walk on eggshells" is a **Red Flag** to be aware of.

Some abusers gaslight using important parts of their victim's history to degrade their *gaslightee*. Every gaslighter needs a "gaslightee" to perform their abusive tactics. **A gaslightee tends to succumb** to whatever the gaslighter says or does to diffuse the tension in hopes of being the savior of the relationship. This can often lead the gaslightee to question their own sanity, which increases their anxiety level.

This method of manipulation occurred in Kendall Ann's relationship when she expressed her fears about her abuser's driving. In the past, she had experienced a life-altering event, a serious car accident, and shared her fears about her past experience with her abuser. Instead of respecting her past experience and fears, he made her feel like she was harming *him* by not trusting his erratic driving. In reality, she should have been the one who was upset, not him.

Self-Doubt

Kendall Ann mentioned that she would doubt the relationship when things got bad, and she would start to retreat emotionally. This uncertainty would quickly dissolve when her abuser morphed back into the man she met and fell in love with. This wavering in behavior presents a different form of gaslighting. Without the positive moments that bonded them as a couple, she may not have stayed in the relationship at all. It is also important to note that these moments of false security are part of the fourth stage of the abuse cycle: the *Calm Phase*. Here, negative days are forgotten, and the temporary *Honeymoon Phase* returns (another **Red Flag**). This phase of tranquility and peace does not come with long-term goals towards change or reconciliation, rather it is an effort to weaken the victim further, ensuring that the victim is attached, committed, and confused.

Examples of gaslighting during the *Calm Phase* can look very positive, making them hard to identify. Gift-giving, agreeing to change or "be better," or doting on the victim's needs are all common examples. These behaviors all appear similar to how many people would try to reconcile in a healthy relationship, but the main difference is the lack of genuine change after these gestures. It is important that these same positive behaviors and gestures are present all the time and not just during times of reconciliation. This is another **Red Flag** behavior – *false promises* of change that continually go unfulfilled.

Destruction of Self-Esteem and Gaslighting

There is perhaps no more effective method of gaslighting as projection, a subconscious defense mechanism where someone defends their own insecurities by denying personal issues and "pushing" them onto someone else. The phrase, "the pot calling the kettle black" provides a perfect understanding of this gaslighting phase. Once someone has experienced emotional abuse through gaslighting, their negatively impacted self-esteem and self-doubt makes it easier for them to believe accusations regarding their character flaws. No one should intentionally want to make you feel bad about yourself or to diminish your self-esteem or self-worth. **No matter what.**

In Kendall Ann's relationship her abuser knew, from the *Love Bombing Phase*, that her intellect and her accomplishments meant a great deal to her. So when she made a mistake with the garbage disposal, her abuser knew the most effective way to hurt her was by shaming her in front of a complete stranger. Then, instead of apologizing, he continued to put her down and called her a moron after the plumber left. This affront to Kendall Ann's self-esteem continued to set the stage for the future emotional abuse that was yet to unfold.

The next stage of gaslighting includes **aligning people against the victim**. The gaslighter will work to make the victim believe that others think they are just as crazy or defective as the gaslighter says. This tactic is neither casual nor passive. Instead it is overtly dismissive and aggressive, making it harder for the victim to believe in themselves. Imagine if you woke up one day, hospitalized, and were told that you had suffered a mental break down and everything you thought happened to you last week was a dream. The effects of a thorough gaslighting regimen can feel almost as disarming. By working to align others against you, it is less likely you will trust others. As a result, it will feel more difficult to reach out, even though asking for help from the people you trust is exactly what is needed.

Your loss of control and power is why the gaslighter does not want you to reach out to others. A gaslighter may try to prevent you from seeking outside support by telling you that others are outright liars. After hearing repeated and audacious lies from the gaslighter, it becomes easier to believe anyone outside your relationship would lie to you – even if they say they love you. Gaslighters try to align with you and misalign you from others, further increasing dependence on the abuser. This isolation makes the impending stages of abuse all the much more dangerous and effective.

If there is one pivotal thing to remember at this stage in a relationship, or if you are reflecting on your past relationship and gaslighting was an issue, it is this: **talk to people you care about and listen to what they have to say.** Get perspectives from others and fact check with yourself and with them. If you are not ready to reach out and delve into your painful experiences, spend time with your inner self through journaling, meditation, or speaking out loud to yourself. Sorting through your feelings can help you regain your reality. Remember: *You are not crazy. You are not broken.*

What I Know Now

1. I have worth.

If I were to title the beginning of the Gaslighting Phase of my relationship with my abuser, it would be, "The Deconstruction of Kendall Ann." The isolation and pain that followed would not have been possible without his talent for minimizing my feelings and making me feel worthless. I was learning to "take his word for it" over my own thoughts, ideas, and feelings. My emotional health and well-being were dependent upon his. I was beginning to lose my self-worth and self-esteem. This set the stage for the horrible, painful and dangerous events soon to follow. In any healthy relationship, you should feel you have worth. Sure, one person in the relationship might know more than the other on certain topics, but you shouldn't feel as though you don't have any value. If you're already prone to having low self-esteem or indulging in negative self-talk, it is vital not to allow your partner to exacerbate those feelings.

2. Find your boundaries and stick to them.

I didn't know what my boundaries or expectations were for relationships. My list of non-negotiables didn't exist except for one: No cheating. Because of this, when something I didn't like happened, I just kept thinking about the good times we had during the Love Bombing phase. *But he can be so sweet*, I'd think as he careened down rural roads, ignoring the speed limits and traffic lights. *Why would I throw away a great relationship because of his driving*? Because it wasn't about the driving! I was communicating boundaries by expressing my fears about his driving and he was outright ignoring them. My abuser made me feel like my boundaries and my desires and needs were insignificant in our relationship. He was critical any time I tried to establish a boundary or express a desire. His negative reaction to my boundary setting made me stop trying all together because I knew my requests would fall on deaf ears. I worried that trying to establish boundaries could jeopardize the relationship if my abuser began to think I was "needy," "critical," or "hard to please."

3. Your partner should be your biggest cheerleader.

Maybe they don't wake you each morning with an actual cheer complete with pom-poms, but you should live most days feeling like they love and support you above all others. If your partner constantly makes you feel bad about yourself, they are not the right person for you. You shouldn't have to worry about being threatened by or compared to their exes. You shouldn't be constantly questioning if the person you're in a relationship with even likes you. *You should know*. If you feel you are sliding across thin ice around your partner and constantly pleasing them for fear of rejection, then there might be some serious issues in your relationship. You should feel confident that the same love and support you provide for your partner is reciprocated. This doesn't only apply to your happy times. You deserve to have a partner who will support and honor you; you should not have to live in fear of being abandoned.

What Do You Know Now?

*This section is intended for you to convey your thoughts,
feelings and reflections on what you learned in the chapter by writing
or using other creative forms of expression.*

Chapter 3

Abuse Of Power

"The greater the power, the more dangerous the abuse."
~ Edmund Burke ~

There was no formal ceremony when I abdicated the power in my relationship to my abuser. Instead, I began noticing I was doing things that were not authentically me. I had gotten so used to choosing behaviors to avoid upsetting my abuser, as opposed to doing what I wanted, I failed to notice that I was slipping into dangerous territory.

I had lived in the city where we met for several years, but because I worked from home and had such strong ties to Maryland, I hadn't made many new friends. I did, however, have one powerful ally who lived nearby, my cousin Christine. Being only three months apart in age, we were inseparable as children and the tales of our antics live on in our family lore today. In the beginning of my relationship with my abuser, I began to see Christine less often. We both attributed this to how busy we were, but as time passed, I missed her. No one could make me laugh quite as hard as Christine, and I desperately needed to find something to giggle about.

Christine and I decided we should meet for dinner one evening and catch up. I was excited to see her smiling face and reconnect. Despite my excitement, telling my abuser about the upcoming dinner did not go as I had hoped. First, he invited himself along. I thought maybe I had been unclear, leading him to believe that he was invited when the dinner was meant for just my cousin and me. Next, he told me it was too dangerous for the two of us to go out in the city alone. I told him I thought his concern was ridiculous and was met with a tearful explanation of how devasted he would be if something were to happen to me and he hadn't done all he could to protect me. He told me he was just so in love with me; he didn't think he could go on if something awful happened to me. It felt nice to have someone so concerned with my safety. I even empathized with him for worrying about me. Not wanting to cause him distress, we compromised. I would still go to dinner, but I would be home promptly at 8:30.

The night of the dinner arrived. As I stood in the bathroom applying my makeup, my abuser leaned on the door jamb. He looked me over. "That's a lot of makeup and quite an outfit to be meeting your cousin," he said with spite, putting air quotes around the words, "your cousin." I looked at my outfit and laughed. I was wearing a sweater and jeans, certainly nothing I would consider overtly sexual or inappropriate.

"Don't laugh at me," he shouted. I was startled.

"There is nothing wrong with this outfit," I said firmly.

"Everyone warned me that you were probably a cheating slut," he shouted as he walked away from the bathroom.

"A what?" I shouted. I chased after him.

What followed was a twenty-minute argument where he accused me of going out to cheat on him instead of meeting my cousin. He cried. He begged me not to leave. He implored me not to break his heart and to stay home. Another compromise: I could go, but I needed to answer the phone by the second ring if he called and reply to any texts within three minutes.

At dinner, Christine and I could barely have a conversation between his calls and texts. I kept apologizing to her. She was gracious, but there was something in her gaze that made me realize what was happening wasn't healthy behavior. Neither of us addressed the elephant in the room and I made sure I was home well before my 8:30 curfew. It would be months before I made plans to see Christine again. The agony of that dinner completely deterred me from wanting to try again.

Soon, my social life consisted of activities solely with my abuser and his family, so I was thrilled when my company's yearly sales conference rolled around. I worked remotely, so I was excited each year when everyone in the company gathered in Dallas to celebrate and to learn about the company's upcoming initiatives. I relished the time I got to spend in person with my coworkers since most of our day-to-day communication was over the phone. The conference had the energy of a fun family reunion with some work intertwined. There was wine, laughter, and comradery, making it more like a vacation than just a work trip.

Weeks before my trip to Dallas, my abuser tried to convince me that it was inappropriate for my company to ask its employees to gather without their significant others. He frequently voiced his discomfort about my traveling without him and drinking wine with other men. He was concerned I was putting myself in a precarious situation where men might behave badly.

His concern evolved into accusing me of wanting to go to Dallas to cheat on him with someone in my company. When I pressed for reasons or a rationale to support his accusations, he couldn't provide any evidence but maintained he knew it was true. Several times, he threatened to break up with me if I went on the trip and told me if I decided to go, I'd find my belongings and Ozzy in the front yard when I returned. I spent countless nights awake, thinking of lies I could tell my boss to get me out of the trip, but I also desperately wanted to go. I wanted to have fun. I wanted to feel good about the success I was having in my job. I wanted to see familiar faces. Again, we struck a bargain. I could go but had to check in frequently and be in bed by 10 pm each night.

When I arrived in Dallas, I felt a rush of independence I hadn't realized I was missing. At night, I found myself rebelling against the rules my abuser had made for me. At 9:55 I would leave the hotel bar where my coworkers were gathering and walk to my hotel room. I would change into my pajamas, take pictures of myself and send them to my abuser. I'd then call my abuser and chat about my day while fake yawning and pretending to be sleepy. When it seemed I had convinced him that I was close to falling asleep, we'd get off the phone. As soon as I ended the call, I'd immediately change back into my clothes and go back to the bar to be with my friends. Most laughed at my antics and cheered as I returned for another glass of Pinot Grigio, but several women seemed concerned. I saw it as nothing more than tapping into my mischievous spirit, something I had been out of touch with for so many months.

35

Although I loved the independence I felt on my work trip, I couldn't maintain it after I returned. When both my abuser and I were at home, my attention was fully committed to him. If I was on the phone when he arrived home from work, I'd immediately hang up so that I could welcome him appropriately. Despite my effort to be attentive, he still told me he was hurt and he felt I was choosing whoever was on the phone over him. I hated to hurt his feelings. I loved him, but shouldn't I be allowed to have others in my life?

After we got engaged, I believed he'd feel more confident about my commitment to him. I figured I'd be able to spend more time with Christine, start dance classes again, and wouldn't have to lie about wanting to be around my friends during my sales conference. I was wrong. Things only got worse. Before I was engaged to my abuser, I traveled home every year to Maryland to see my family for either Thanksgiving, Christmas, or both. Now, I was ecstatic about returning from the big city to show off my fiancé and to revel in the bliss of my engagement with my family.

"I can't wait to show everyone my engagement ring!" I squealed one early November evening. "Do you want to go to Maryland with me for Thanksgiving or Christmas? Do you feel like you'd rather stay here for one in particular because I am fine with just going home for one and I don't care which one!"

There was a long pause.

"I can't believe you'd leave me during the holidays," he said through tears.

"I'm not leaving you. You're coming with me!" I replied happily.

"Kendall Ann, I am your family now and if you'd rather spend your holidays with other people, you really should give me the ring back." He began to cry.

My stomach dropped. "I'll stay here with you," I whispered.

We spent Thanksgiving with his family who lived locally. It hurt and confused me that he thought I was betraying him by wanting to be around my family for the holidays, but the same rules didn't apply to him. Then on Christmas morning I sat on the bathroom floor and sobbed as *Have Yourself A Merry Little Christmas* echoed through the house. It dawned on me that maybe I was sacrificing more in the relationship than I was getting in return.

After we were engaged, I noticed how difficult it became to find any personal space away from my fiancé. If I wanted to read or talk on the phone, he'd make excuses to be in the same room. These were always flimsy excuses, but ones I couldn't argue with. These intrusions continued when I was showering in the bathroom. He would come into the bathroom to ask me questions, rolling open the door to the shower without even asking, leaving me standing in front of him nude. It made me deeply uncomfortable and I asked him several times to stop. He laughed it off and told me that he'd seen me naked a thousand times, so I should stop being "insecure." Since there was no lock on the bathroom door, I did my best to avoid showering while he was home.

One day after working out, I had to shower. He came into the bathroom and looked in the linen closet. He remarked that he hadn't found what he was looking for and left the room abruptly. I was relieved he hadn't opened the shower door. I got out of the shower and began my routine of drying off, applying lotion, and then putting back on my engagement ring that I kept on a ring stand in the linen closet. When I went to put on my ring, it wasn't on the stand. My heart sank to the floor.

Where is my ring?

I tore through the house looking for it. When my search yielded nothing, I walked into the living room where he sat on the couch.

"You didn't happen to take my ring from the closet, did you?" I asked sheepishly.

"No!" He yelled. "Oh my God, is the ring lost? It's so expensive, Kendall Ann! I didn't get the chance to get insurance on it yet."

That was news to me. I burst into tears.

"We'll find it," he said jumping from the couch.

We searched for at least ten minutes with no luck. I was devastated. I couldn't believe I had lost the ring. How could I have been so stupid? And no insurance. I had lost us a fortune.

"Found it!" he shouted as he ran towards me, ring in hand.

I fell to floor in relief. "Thank you so much. Oh my God. Where did you find it?" I inquired.

"Stuck in the sofa cushions," he responded.

Strange. I hadn't been in the living room for very long that day before I took a shower. It was possible it fell off but not probable. I felt a wrenching in my gut. I had no idea if he had taken the ring from the closet or if I had truly lost it. Immediately I rejected the idea that he had taken the ring. *Why would he do that? That is just too strange. Would he purposely make me anxious? No.* But something inside me whispered, *maybe.*

The next day as I placed the ring in the ring stand before my shower, I paused. I wrapped my towel around me and walked out of the bathroom into the spare bedroom, which was my office. I grabbed a pen, peeled off a bright pink Post-it, and wrote, "Your ring is here." I went back into the bathroom and placed the note on top of my ring. I did the same thing every time I showered from then on, just in case.

A similar type of deception occurred again when my mom came to visit so we could go wedding dress shopping. The first evening she arrived we sat with my fiancé, sipping wine and talking.

"Kendall Ann, I can't believe you were able to bring your plant back to life," she said pointing to a large potted plant in the corner of the room.

It was the same plant she had given me when I moved into my first apartment alone. The plant was a cutting from a plant she still had, and it always reminded me of our connection even as I lived hundreds of miles from her. I never had a green thumb and many times the plant was near death, but I always found a way to bring it back from the brink.

"It's alive because of me," my fiancé chimed in.

I laughed. "No, it's not."

"Yes, it is. I water it every day." He lied.

"I have never seen you water it and if you were watering it that much, it would be dead."

Silence engulfed the room.

I read the confusion on my mom's face. "Well, I am just glad it's still alive," she noted, trying to cut the tension.

My stomach twisted. *What is he doing? Why would he lie like that? Is he trying to make himself look good in front of my mother? To impress her? Is he trying to make me look like I didn't care about the plant she gave me?* It was strange. The cloud of confusion settled on me once again.

That wasn't his only odd behavior during the visit. While watching television we saw an advertisement for a deep discount from the store where he had recently purchased his suit for our upcoming wedding.

"We should go and see if they can do a price adjustment," I suggested.

"That's a great idea," my mom replied.

"The store is right near a great restaurant. How about we go tonight before dinner?" my fiancé suggested.

That evening we stopped by the store and they agreed to discount the suit. The three of us toasted our great luck at dinner.

"Getting the discount was such a great idea," he said to my mom after the toast.

"But it was my idea!," I blurted out.

"Nice try, Kendall Ann," he said, his words dripping in condescension. "Don't take credit for your mom's idea."

My mom and I looked at each other knowingly. It wasn't worth ruining an evening over, but it left me feeling unsettled.

That night as I lay in bed next to him, my mind wandered back to what had happened. *Why is he lying about things like watering plants? Is he trying to be nice to my mother by giving her credit for my idea? Does he think it really was her idea and is he too stubborn to consider the possibility that he was wrong? Why am I letting a plant and a suit wind me up?*

I couldn't stand lying next to him. Ozzy followed me as I quietly retreated to the couch in the living room. I set my alarm for early the next day so there was no chance of my mom seeing me on the couch. I did not want to be questioned. I cried as I lay there consumed by the thought that I couldn't even stand to be in the same bed as my fiancé on the weekend I was buying my wedding dress. What was I going to do?

The Power of Isolation

There is safety in numbers. Isolation is an essential factor in establishing control in an abusive relationship. We gain our confidence in the face of adversity when we have others alongside us. Though we all desire differing sizes of personal communities, we are all innately social beings. We need people. For an abuser to shift the power of a relationship in their favor, they must work to reduce the strength of their partner's social support. The fewer people their partner can call on, talk to, or reach out to, the better. If you find that you have stopped seeing friends and family due to your relationship, that is a **Red Flag**. A healthy relationship should be able to integrate into other relationships you already have as opposed to separating you from those you love.

A lack of self-worth may have been the motivator for why Kendall Ann's abuser felt the need to attain power by isolating her. This was evident in the insecure way he reacted whenever she wanted to spend time with anyone who was not him. If she intended to be around someone of the opposite sex, even a co-worker, he insisted she was cheating. If she wanted to spend time with her family (for instance, her cousin, her closest confidant and friend), he assumed she was lying about the company she was keeping and reacted in anger and jealousy. He always found a reason to defy or doubt her intentions whenever she tried to spend time with anyone who might give her support. His efforts to instill guilt were a very effective attempt at establishing control, not only over whom she spent her time with but also regarding *how* she spent her time.

In a healthy, non-abusive relationship there is no need to be the sole focus in someone's life. Conversely, in an unhealthy relationship the need to isolate a significant other stems from the fear that their partner will see who the abuser really is and leave. Fear of abandonment is a common motivator for those who try to isolate their victims. This fear can lead abusers too use jealousy as a weapon, which Kendall Ann's abuser did on more than one occasion. He weaponized isolation and jealousy by targeting Kendall Ann's sensitivity and compassion. Displays of *jealousy through isolation* is one of the **Red Flags** to be mindful of when assessing your own relationship.

The Power of Control Wheel

Many of the tactics used by her abuser can be found in the *Power of Control Wheel*. The Power of Control Wheel was developed by Domestic Abuse Intervention Programs in 1981, a group run by activists in Duluth, MN, that received contributions from American sociologist, Ellen Pence. Learning the different parts of the wheel is crucial when trying to determine whether your own relationship has concerning or abusive qualities.

On the following pages you will find the eight different categories in the Power of Control Wheel. These categories include using coercion or threats, using intimidation, using emotional abuse, using isolation, minimizing, denial and blaming, using children, using male privilege (the LGBT model is featured as well for reference in case this model does not fit your relationship), and using economic abuse. Not all pieces of the wheel need to be present in a relationship to classify the relationship as abusive or unhealthy. In fact, only ***one single category*** needs to be identified for the relationship to be considered potentially abusive. Often if a relationship is abusive, one trait will evolve into additional forms of abuse the longer the relationship continues. It is important to realize that thinking things will "get better" in an abusive relationship is unlikely. Instead it is *more* likely that the relationship will become more abusive.

Be aware, relationships go through difficulties and at times issues with power and control can occur even in non-abusive relationships. Acute or chronic stress in a relationship can increase the likelihood that a couple will struggle with some of the issues found in this wheel. It is crucial to examine whether the piece of the chart that applies to your relationship has started to make you feel **disconnected from who you are or a lack of overall safety**. *Disconnection from Self* is another **Red Flag**. If this occurs, then the power of control issue presenting is likely not due to situational stress or hardship. Rather it may represent a sign that the relationship is heading in a dangerous direction.

In the beginning of this chapter, Kendall Ann said she was starting to feel like she wasn't being her authentic self. If she had seen the Power of Control Wheel in the early stages of her relationship, she might have recognized other looming issues. You can find the models of the wheel on the following pages to reflect on potential issues present in your own current or past relationship.

41

The Power of Control Wheel

Power of Control Wheel for LGBT Relationships

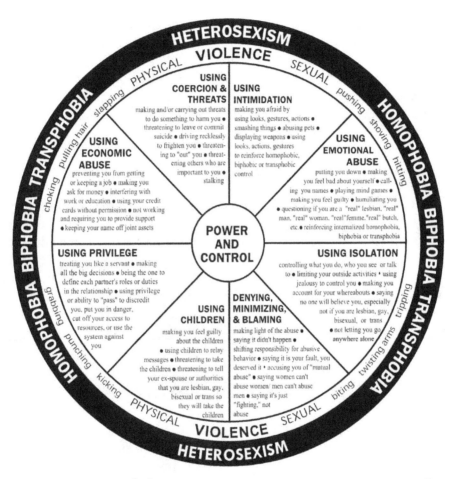

Developed by Roe & Jagodinsky

3

A Slippery Slope

After reviewing the Power of Control Wheel, do you see any pieces matching your relationship? Further, are there any you fear could potentially become a problem in the future? It is important to ask these questions when exploring your relationship, because power and control in an abusive relationship works in a progressive manner. These traits often present themselves gradually, making it difficult to anticipate how severe the abuse can become. As discussed in the section on *Love Bombing* in **Chapter 1**, it would be difficult to accomplish the manipulation and degradation of someone's persona if the abuser started the relationship with severe forms of abuse. Rather, abuse is often a slow, methodical build.

In addition to using isolation, Kendall Ann's abuser used *emotional abuse* in its many forms to manipulate her. He tried to instill doubt in Kendall Ann by playing mind games and "making her think she was crazy." He did this when he hid the engagement ring to cause emotional stress. He refused to give her credit for simple accomplishments: the idea for the wedding suit and keeping her mother's plant alive. He also inflicted guilt on her when she wanted to spend time with others and worked hard to make her feel bad about herself. He refused to encourage her to spend time with family and friends for the holidays and even made her feel bad about such requests.

Abuse of Power and Substance Abuse

When exploring abuse of power it is important to mention the potential connection to substance abuse. Research shows that substance abuse can be a precipitating event for many instances of intimate partner violence, and it can usually intensify the severity of violence. Often times, interventions for substance abuse have proven successful in reducing instances of violence. Violence is less likely to occur if substance abuse issues are addressed.

At times, substance abuse can also be used as a method of power and control. Some abusers coerce their partners to reduce self-efficacy and independence through the use of illicit drugs. This can create greater economic and emotional dependence on the abuser. If you feel you have been coerced into using drugs or alcohol, or that your use is problematic, we encourage you to seek support. Some options include; Alcoholics Anonymous and other 12-Step programs, Yoga for 12-Step Recovery (Y12SR), SMART Recovery, or Refuge Recovery which utilizes mindfulness, meditation, and Buddhist principles. All of these groups have both online and in-person options.

Abuse of Power Self-Assessment

It is important in any relationship to be aware of any potential abuse of power. Taking a closer look can help identify unhealthy or abusive relationships before they become dangerous. We encourage you to use the Power of Control Wheel to identify any pieces that apply to your own relationship and explore them further with the journal prompts on the following page.

If writing in the book does not feel safe, we understand. It is not uncommon to be concerned with privacy when experiencing abuse. This feeling does not go away just because the relationship may be ending; it can take time. So, whether you journal here, or just make mental notes, we encourage you to identify any potential problems, hopefully before they start to get any worse.

45

Power of Control Journal Entry

When looking at the Power of Control Wheel and reflecting on my own relationship I notice:

What I Know Now

1. Do you miss yourself? If so, you're probably not in the right relationship.

I used to think that the phrase "acting out of character" was meaningless. I now realize I was so far away from my authentic self in my relationship that my actions did not reflect the person I am which was certainly "acting out of character." Abandoning my friends? Ignoring my family? Lying to my partner so I could hang out with my coworkers? That was never who I had been, and it was not the person I wanted to be. My relationship wasn't making me evolve into a better person, rather I was turning into someone I did not recognize. You should not have to sacrifice the person you are for the person that your partner wants you to be. There is room for everyone to improve in some way, but if you are having to make sweeping changes to yourself simply to please your partner, you might not be in the right relationship.

2. Don't give up the people who "knew you when."

It's natural to get caught up in the excitement of a new relationship and to spend time with your new love, but at some point, things go back to normal. If your partner resists your desire to remain connected with the other people in the world who love you and know you best, then something is wrong. Your partner should want to enhance your life and not want to be the only person in it. If your relationships with your family and friends are an important facet of your life, it helps to make that clear in any relationship. If they cannot handle "sharing" you with the other people who are important to you, it might be a sign that there will be other boundaries they won't respect. It is easier for your partner to control you when you're isolated from those who may have an opinion about how your partner behaves.

3. Damn, I didn't realize he financially abused me too.

At one point in my relationship, I interviewed for a new job. I wasn't completely sold on the opportunity, but as soon as my interviewer told me I'd have to entertain clients by attending sports events and dinners, I knew it was a no. Not because I minded these things, but because I imagined the hell my abuser would put me through if I had to spend time away from him. When I turned down the job, the employer offered me a significantly higher salary to change my mind. That night I told my abuser I was considering taking the job because of the money, but the new position meant my abuser would be alone some evenings.

"I didn't think you'd be the kind of person who would sacrifice your relationship for money," he said and walked out of the room. I didn't take the job. I now know that my abuser was trying to make sure I didn't have enough independence to leave him, and one way to control me was to control the amount of money I made. The less money I made, the less likely I'd be to leave him for fear I couldn't make it on my own.

What Do You Know Now?

*This section is intended for you to convey your thoughts,
feelings and reflections on what you learned in the chapter by writing
or using other creative forms of expression.*

Chapter 4

Verbal Abuse

"A tongue has no bones, but is strong enough to break a heart."
~ Proverbs 15:1 ~

"Mom, do most couples fight a lot before their wedding?" I whispered into my phone a month before I was supposed to get married.

"What do you mean?" my mom responded.

I was silent. I didn't want to repeat the awful things my fiancé had yelled at me the night before.

"We're just not really getting along right now," I said trying to sugarcoat the truth.

My mom explained that weddings can often be stressful for people. She told me that many couples argue more than normal in the months before their wedding because of the stress. It was hard to tell if she really believed what she was saying, or if she was just trying to calm my nerves.

Something churned inside of me. I was desperate to tell the truth about what was going on, but I was scared. What if I told my mom what my fiancé said, and it made her hate him? I was already keeping so many secrets about our relationship. What was one more?

"He said, 'Fuck you, stupid bitch,' last night when we were arguing," I blurted out into the phone.

Silence.

"Mom?" I asked.

"I'm thinking," my mom replied. More silence. Finally, she

51

spoke. "Kendall Ann, all I can tell you is this: Your father and I were married for twenty-nine years and he never called me a bitch."

I swallowed hard and told her I needed to go but I loved her and I would call her back.

It had been months since my abuser and I had been able to disagree on something without it spiraling into yelling, cursing, and name calling. Admittedly, sometimes I was doing the yelling to be heard and I said things I wasn't proud of.

The screaming and nasty words weren't present at the beginning, but over time he was saying things that were wounding me deeply. I've always been self-conscious about my weight, a concern I had revealed to my abuser early in our relationship. At the time, he had reacted with kind words about how he thought I was beautiful. Then, things changed.

"Are you sure you want to wear those shorts?" he asked one morning as we prepared to leave the house.

"Yeah," I answered.

"Oh okay. It's just that you said you are uncomfortable with how big your legs are, so I am surprised," he answered.

"Are you saying my legs look big?" I questioned with pain in my voice.

"I'm just repeating what you had said!" he exclaimed. "I'm just looking out for you."

I paused. It seemed like he had just said my legs looked fat. Maybe I was reading too much into it. Still, it made me uncomfortable. I went into the room and changed into jeans.

Soon after, while lying on the couch together I rolled over onto him to give him a kiss.

"Ugh," he uttered.

"Am I squishing you?" I asked playfully.

"No. I just wasn't expecting you to weigh so much."

I looked at him with my mouth agape.

"I'm just used to my ex and she was just..." his voice trailed off.

"She was just much smaller than you."

His words cut me deeply. Whether he had said the exact words or not, he had just implied that I was fatter than his ex and it hurt.

As our relationship progressed, the casual remarks about my

weight continued, and he began criticizing the amount I ate and how I looked in my clothes. One night his comments became not quite as casual. We were in the middle of an argument and before he walked out of the room, I heard his hateful words,

"Whatever, fat ass."

I was too stunned to reply. From then on, he mentioned "fat" and its various synonyms whenever he was upset with me. These remarks tormented me, and I began restricting what I ate and started exercising daily. Still the hurtful words about my body continued. When I said I wanted to try paddle boarding for the first time on our upcoming honeymoon, he told me that paddle boarding was for "athletes" and I would not be able to do such a vigorous sport. The lowest point in his body shaming came during intimacy, when he pinched the fat on my stomach and told me I still had "some work to do." His degrading comments were not only centered around my weight. He was becoming highly critical about other aspects of my appearance as well.

One warm fall evening his parents invited us to their house for dinner because some out-of-town relatives were visiting. I had just splurged on a Michael Kors, safari-inspired khaki dress and I was excited to show it off. I put it on and gazed in the mirror, loving the way it looked. I felt confident.

"You look like you work at the zoo," he said as I slid on my platform sandals.

"It's trendy!" I said laughing. "You don't get it because you're a boy!" I added teasingly.

"You can't wear that to my parents. It's embarrassing," he snapped.

"It's very stylish and I feel good in it," I answered.

"You look fucking stupid. Everyone is going to make fun of you. If you want to wear that, you can't come."

"But I love this dress and it makes me happy."

"And if you don't go, then I can't go because everyone will wonder where you are and I'll have to lie because I can't tell them that you are so selfish that you'd pick wearing an ugly dress over seeing my family," he said crossing his arms.

I felt stuck, but the real Kendall Ann roared inside of me.

"This is what I am wearing," I answered calmly. "Now let's go."

He flicked off his shoes and stomped toward the closet.

"Might as well change into something comfortable since I have to be stuck in this house because you won't change. You're so selfish that you'd block me from seeing people I love. What kind of a person are you?"

"The kind of person who wears what she likes and doesn't get bullied," I responded.

He turned toward me and paused. He took a deep breath. "I think we should break up. I don't want to be with someone who intentionally keeps me away from my family. This is very controlling and manipulative, and I don't feel comfortable being in a relationship with someone who treats me like that."

"Are you insane?" I screeched. "I am dressed and ready to go hang out with your family. You're the one who is refusing to go because you don't like my outfit. You're not even making sense."

"I can't believe how mean you are! Making me choose between my family who I love and you. It's like you want me all to yourself!" he shouted back.

My head was spinning. I was so confused. *What were we even arguing about? How did he have this so twisted. He was the one saying we were no longer going to a dinner, not me.* He walked into the closet and reappeared with one of my suitcases.

"Start packing your shit," he said throwing the suitcase on the bed. "We're finished. I can't be with someone so selfish."

I stared at him confused.

"Go!" he screamed.

"I think we need some space," I whispered. Ozzy and I hopped in my car and drove around for an hour. I stopped for food and ate alone on a bench in the park, Ozzy lying at my feet. I tried to think through what had happened. *Am I wrong? Should I have changed? Am I being stubborn for no reason?* I drove home and walked into the bedroom. A note rested on my pillow. "I'm sorry. I love you," it read. I slipped off my dress and hung it in the closet, running my fingertips along its buttons.

I found him lying on the couch in the living room. I gently lay on top of him. He hugged me tightly and kissed my forehead.

"I love you," he whispered softly.

"I love you, too," I replied.

We never talked about what happened and sadly; I never wore that dress again.

When he wasn't criticizing my appearance or calling my ideas "stupid" or "worthless" during arguments and discussions, he employed the silent treatment if I disagreed with him. He would go hours ignoring me when he knew I was upset with him. I, of course, would become frustrated with his lack of communication and would lash out or beg him to speak to me. Expressing my feelings resulted in his calling me "crazy," "irrational," or "mentally ill." The original argument would often be forgotten and over shadowed by his insults. Instead of addressing the real issues, I would then spend my time trying to convince him that I was, in fact, none of those things.

His sarcasm became a daily part of life and I began to avoid bringing up issues in our relationship in hopes of avoiding his harsh words. If I criticized him in any way he would respond with snide remarks like, "Oh of course I will immediately change. I forgot that you're perfect so I should do everything you say." If I continued to disagree with him, I would be told things like, "I'm trying to make this as easy as possible for you to understand, but I really can't dumb it down for you anymore." Even the simplest requests were met with condescension, so I stopped bringing up any topic or point he might disagree with all together.

Soon even my smallest actions were criticized. According to him, my mom had not taught me how to fold laundry correctly and my makeup made me look like a clown. My accent was "annoying" to most people and I was "brainless" for wanting to go to church. Everything about me was up for attack. Over time I learned that the best way to protect myself from his vicious words was to simply change. I found myself asking for his guidance on how to do everything. "How would you like me to fold the laundry?" I'd inquire and then listen intently to get every detail.

Better yet, if I could anticipate what might make him upset or critical, I would change proactively to avoid his brutal criticism and punishment. I was always rewarded for such behavior. He'd shower me with compliments about how beautiful and smart I was. He would tell me that he never met someone as hard working, loving, and loyal as I was. He loved the way I treated our dogs with such care and kindness, and he was so proud to be engaged to me.

For weeks we'd be in what I thought was a good place. We were kind, loving, and supportive towards each other – facing the world together as a team. Then, I'd do something "moronic," "idiotic," or "braindead" such as not cleaning up muddy footprints the dogs had left in the kitchen quickly enough. I'd kneel on the floor cleaning up the mess and wonder if maybe I was as "stupid," "fat," and "annoying" as he told me I was.

The Power of Verbal Abuse

Words are powerful. They have the ability to shape and define what we believe about ourselves and our world. Verbal abuse can be quiet and subtle; or it can be obvious, loud, or violent. Some people have the misconception that verbal abuse is not as harmful as physical abuse. I have worked with victims of verbal abuse that excuse the behavior of their abuser by saying that the abuser was *only* yelling at them or berating them verbally, not physically hurting them. Since there was no physical harm, responsibility for harm was not properly assigned to the abuser. Using misnomers like *"only"* or *"at least"* are permissive attitudes towards verbal abuse that need to **stop**.

The negative ramifications of verbal abuse and aggression can lead to harmful side-effects, such as physical illness or internalized reenactments of the abuse in the form of self-harm. It is important to understand that the brain cannot differentiate between physical and emotional pain. This form of abuse is serious, and it is crucial to take a stand for your right to safety and respect. Verbal abuse should never become a norm in your relationship. The longer verbal abuse occurs, the harder it is to stop it. The very nature of this form of abuse is that it can slowly erode self-worth of its victim, making it harder to stand up for oneself and leave the relationship. There are a number of forms of verbal abuse that presented in Kendall Ann's relationship. Some of these included:

- Name Calling
- Condescension
- Criticism
- Degradation
- Manipulation
- Blame
- Accusations
- Withholding or Isolation
- Gaslighting
- Circular Arguments
- Threats

Kendall Ann attempted to set boundaries by speaking up for herself during arguments with her abuser. When this didn't work she took time away with her beloved dog, Ozzy, and questioned the health of her relationship. Ending the relationship appeared to be the only way to stop the verbal abuse, but Kendall Ann was not ready to leave at this point. Making the choice to leave can be extremely difficult, however you have the right to end your relationship at any point. Leaving asserts your power that you will not tolerate verbal abuse. Leaving an abuser will protect one of the most precious aspects of your physiology: your brain.

The Brain on Verbal Abuse

What happens to the brain when someone is being verbally abused? Neuroimaging experiments, including research out of the University of Michigan, have been conducted examining whether the circuitry of the brain that reads pain can decipher between emotional or physical pain. These studies show that the same parts of the brain light up when experiencing the pain of lost love, rejection, or memories of conflict, as when physical pain is experienced. What this means is that verbal abuse should *not* be viewed as a "less severe" form of abuse simply because it lacks physical endangerment. Instead of external scars, the damage manifests in the brain and affects the way we think, feel, and experience our world.

Studies conducted on children exposed to emotional and verbal abuse reveal the detrimental impact of such actions. Research shows that the presence of emotional abuse permanently alters a child's brain by enhancing the mechanisms in the brain intended for survival. Verbally abused children must learn to adapt to their environment. If a child grows up in emotional chaos, the parts of the brain related to stress, fear, self-protection, hypervigilance, and mistrust are reinforced while the areas of the brain hardwired to cope with interpersonal stress and trusting others weaken. This explains why victims of abuse who are slowly gaslit and manipulated tend to cope with the stress of a negative relationship better than someone who has not experienced abuse in the past-because it is familiar. For this reason, those who have experienced developmental trauma in their past may stay longer in abusive relationships than those

58

who have not been normalized to such stress.

You may have heard the adage: "Throw a frog in a pot of boiling water, it will hop right out. But if you put that frog in a pot of tepid water and slowly warm it, the frog will not figure out what is going on until it's too late."[3]

The saying exemplifies how gaslighting and emotional abuse works. You may not realize it is happening until it is too late.

Silence

Silence is a form of "non-verbal" abuse, or covert punishment, that Kendall Ann described her abuser using as an abuse tactic when he was angry and trying to inflict punishment. When silence is used in an abusive manner, it is intended to change the behavior of its victim without appearing overtly manipulative. There are times where silence may be used as a trauma response or a form of self-protection, but if it is being used to inflict pain or isolation on its victim, it is not a form of coping, but rather a form of manipulation. You can determine whether silence is abusive as opposed to a trauma response if the abuser is resistant to change or defensive about their silence. In that case it is more likely that the silence is intended to control and punish as opposed to being for personal protection.

Gottman Method

There are various theories regarding self-protection in romantic relationships. The Gottman Method is an approach to couples' therapy that includes a thorough assessment of romantic relationships and integrates research-based interventions based on the Sound Relationship House Theory. Gottman Method explores the use of silence between couples referred to as **stonewalling**. *Stonewalling* is another **Red Flag** found in abusive relationships. According to the Gottman Institute, stonewalling occurs (whether in a discussion or an argument) when the listener with-draws from the interaction, shuts down and closes themselves off from the speaker because they are feeling overwhelmed or physiologically

---

3   This pithy concept is attributed to Stephenie Meyer.

flooded- which is when emotions become too overwhelming and produce an influx of emotions that become too overwhelming and produce an influx in physiological sensations and stress hormones such as adrenaline and cortisol. Metaphorically speaking, the stonewaller builds a wall between themselves and their partner. Rather than confronting issues, the person who is stonewalling will be totally unresponsive and make evasive maneuvers such as tuning out, turning away, acting busy, or engaging in obsessive behaviors.

Learning about how your partner responds to emotional flooding, or the inability to process emotions either physically or mentally, can help to improve conflict resolution. The problem in an emotionally abusive relationship however is that the stonewaller will not be willing to explore issues and may even gaslight their partner into thinking there is something wrong with *them* as opposed to taking responsibility for their own issues and need for growth.

This behavior was seen in Kendall Ann's relationship when her abuser refused to go to dinner at his parents' house as a means to punish her for embarrassing him. He was not only emotionally abusing her by putting her down and demeaning her physical appearance, but he was also gaslighting her by blaming her for not being able to go out for the evening. His own insecurities and need to control her were the issues at hand, not her beautiful dress and desire to be independent.

Negative Self-Talk

Emotional abuse, both verbal and through silence, degrades the victim's ego strengths. Using positive self-talk helps to rebuild this strength and restore one's natural resilience. Being trapped in a relationship where you experience abuse; emotionally, physically, financially, or through other power and control means, can result in using problematic coping skills to survive. Self-blame is an example of this, which can lead to internalizing abuse. There were many times in Kendall Ann's story where she questioned if her abuser's insulting comments were true. He convinced her that she was to blame for most conflicts they had, even if he was the one who instigated it.

Self-doubt and hyper-focusing on one's own flaws are also common thinking patterns of depression. *Depression* often manifests as *anger turned inwards* and is usually accompanied by negative self-talk.

When evaluating the health of your relationship, be aware of *negative self-talk,* which is a **Red Flag**. This thinking pattern was certainly present for Kendall Ann when she blamed herself and made excuses for her abuser when trying to understand his verbal abuse.

One way individuals may try to cope with anger turned inwards is through numbing the pain with substance use. Substance abuse, is another **Red Flag**. Substance use appears to *take the edge off,* but it does not heal or change anything. Substances are a quick way to bring **relief**, but they do not bring **resolution**. Numbing the pain of abuse may make one event seem a bit more bearable, but whatever pain led to the drink, or other substance of choice, will be present tomorrow. In Kendall Ann's case, her methods of numbing were disordered eating, negative self-talk, and codependency.

Dialectical Behavior Therapy (DBT) Skills

A healthier way to deal with the negative impact that verbal abuse can have is with Dialectical Behavioral Therapy (DBT) which provides a number of conflict resolution skills designed to improve interpersonal effectiveness. DBT was developed by Marsha M. Linehan as a form of cognitive-behavioral therapy, or talk therapy, to help people establish healthier reactions to intense emotions and situations. The four main modules found in this treatment take approximately 24-weeks to complete and can be done in a group or individual setting:

1. Mindfulness
2. Interpersonal Effectiveness
3. Distress Tolerance
4. Emotion Regulation

The modules include homework that is often processed in a formal group with a DBT aware therapist. For the purpose of helping you on your journey towards thriving, we would like to provide two skills that can help if you are currently in an unhealthy relationship or trying to survive the aftermath of one. The first skill is in the interpersonal effectiveness module. It is called the **DEAR MAN** skill.

DEAR MAN

DEAR MAN is an interpersonal effectiveness skill designed to improve the way you communicate with others, especially when confronting or engaging in conflict. This skill is an acronym for:

Describe the situation and stick to the facts. Use observations such as "I notice," "I see," or "I hear" supplemented with specifics about the situation. Be aware not to add too much detail centered on non-related issues as you can quickly derail your efforts and lose your message.

Express your feelings, often using an "I" statement. For example, use the phrase, "I feel." Be careful not to use "I feel" about an accusation, such as "I feel you are being disrespectful." Rather, use "I feel disrespected." If you own your feelings there is no refuting them. On the other hand, an accusation can be argued, usually with the person you are trying to confront.

Assert means to ask for what you want or to say **"no"** very clearly. Examples of how to start asserting yourself: "I would like," "I would rather," or "Can you please?" Notice, none of these statements are aggressive in manner. There is a misconception that conflict is an aggressive interaction. On the contrary, conflicts (or DEAR MANs) work better if they are *clear* and not aggressive.

Reinforce the positives that can come out of the person's listening, changing, or at least understanding your position and/ or statements. Point out how much better your relationship may become if they understand your needs and desires.

Mindfully: Keep the focus on what you want and centered on how you are feeling in the moment. If you feel you are getting distracted or thrown off by the other person, you can go back to your original assertion using the "broken record" skill and repeat what you want. This is especially important to remember if the person you are talking to attempts to derail your message or attacks you. Remember, not many people are trained in DBT skills or know how to use DEAR MAN, so their skills will not necessarily match yours in a conflict. You have an appropriate advantage – use it.

If you feel disconnected from your body during the conflict (for some this feels like the beginning stages of panic), come back to your breath. You cannot breathe in the **past** and you cannot breathe in the *future*; you can only breathe in the **present** and that is exactly where you want to be.

Appearing Confident: Projecting confidence can be really hard if you are up against someone who intimidates you or makes you feel unsafe. If you feel safe, make eye contact, assert yourself (as mentioned before), and stick with what you want to say. Making your voice audible and holding your body in a power posture help to emphasize your stance further.

Negotiate: There are often opposing views in times of conflict, but you can stick to your original assertion while still being open to compromise and negotiation. When using this skill with an abusive person, narcissist, or someone who is already masterful at manipulation, it is imperative not to move away from your original request unless you feel the proposed compromise is true to your needs and desires.

It can be helpful to practice using DEAR MAN with a trusted person. Role playing what you may want to say can help increase confidence in trying the skill, especially for the first time. If there is someone you feel you can trust, or perhaps someone you have been isolated from that you could reconnect with, this is a great time to do so. If you prefer not to include anyone else when practicing the skill, you can certainly role-play this or journal a script on your own.

What if it Does Not Work?

Remember, not everyone knows about DEAR MAN. Just because you possess the skills does not mean the person you are in conflict with has them. It is important not to give up or to give in just because you do not get the feedback you want. One of the tenets of interpersonal effectiveness taught in DBT therapy is to eliminate your expectations of others by using skills of mindfulness in the here and now.

When facing a conflict with an abuser, narcissist, or other highly volatile or resistant personality, the DEAR MAN skill may not be as useful. If you try it with your partner on more than one occasion and it does not go well, indications point to an extreme abuse of power and emotional abuse is likely present.

63

Distress Tolerance

Distress tolerance is another module in DBT that can help you cope with the negative impact emotional and verbal abuse inflicts on the mind, body and soul. We all have experienced distress in our lives to varying degrees. DBT distress tolerance skills are incredibly empowering and can provide relief from common forms of stress such as; work, traffic, relationship issues with friends and family, or financial concerns. These skills increase the ability to handle strong emotional responses to crisis and can reduce the likelihood of you responding in a fight, flight, freeze, or fawn trauma reaction. Below you will learn how to implement **TIPP,** one of the many distress tolerance skills taught in the 24-week DBT skills training.

TIPP

Enduring the stress and pain of an abusive relationship can push you towards your breaking point. The DBT distress tolerance skill, TIPP, is designed to move you away from that emotional ledge. TIPP stands for *Temperature, Intense Exercise, Paced Breathing, and Paired Muscle Relaxation.*

Temperature

When we're upset, our bodies often feel hot. As a countermeasure, splash your face with cold water, hold an ice cube, or let the car's AC blow on your face. Changing your body temperature will help you cool down both physically and emotionally.

Intense Exercise

Do intense exercise to match your intense emotion. You're not a marathon runner? That's okay; you don't need to be. Sprint down to the end of the street, jump in the pool for a few laps, or do jumping jacks until you've tired yourself out. Increasing oxygen flow helps decrease stress levels. Plus, it's hard to stay dangerously upset when you're exhausted.

Paced Breathing

Even something as simple as controlling your breath can have a profound impact on emotional pain. There are many different types of breathing exercises. If you have a favorite, breathe it out. If you don't, try a technique called "box breathing." Each breath interval will be four seconds long. *Take in air for four seconds, hold it in four seconds, breathe out four, and hold for four.* Then start again. Continue to focus on your breathing pattern until you feel calmer. Steady breathing reduces your body's fight or flight response.

Paired Muscle Relaxation

The science of paired muscle relaxation is fascinating. When you tighten a voluntary muscle, relax it, and allow it to rest, the muscle will become more relaxed than it was before. Relaxed muscles require less oxygen; your breathing and heart rate will slow down.

Try this technique by focusing on a group of muscles, such as in your arms. Tighten the muscles as much as you can for five seconds. Then let go of the tension. Let the muscles relax, and you'll begin to relax, as well.

Where to From Here?

Equipped with new skills for handling distress, our hope is that you will experience less stress and perhaps be moving towards a healthier and safer life. Perhaps you are starting to see potential risk factors in your own relationship or are better able to understand what went wrong in a past relationship. It is incredibly difficult to make the final decision to leave an abuser. Changing your entire life, uprooting yourself and possibly your children (if you have a family) can prove unsettling and scary. It is very common for an abuser to threaten to hurt themselves, you, or your children if you try to leave. Manipulation is a powerful tool and having additional support can help to reduce its power. If you are starting to contemplate leaving, we want to support your journey. The planning stages of leaving can take time, courage, and support.

If reading this chapter has shed light on your own experiences with verbal abuse, we encourage you to consider that self-preservation be your new goal. As we learned, verbal abuse is just as harmful, painful, and unacceptable as any other form of abuse. These painful experiences do not always result in physical evidence, but they can be forever imprinted on your heart and mind. Verbal abuse is not something that fades away easily. It is in fact, a mental injury. You should never have to endure belligerent, manipulative, or spiteful words from someone with whom you chose to share your life.

This can be difficult to believe if you have become accustomed to the abuse or endured similar circumstances as a child. Growing up with examples of unstable "love" from a parent or caregiver, or watching parents treat one another with verbal disrespect, have a lasting effect on how you see relationships. In addition to abuse in the home, studies show that children who are bullied in school endure similar emotional injuries, especially if they are too afraid or embarrassed to share details of the bullying with a trusted adult. Much like a child experiencing bullying or abuse, you deserve to speak up for yourself and create a safe and bountiful life. By simply reading this book you are choosing to rewrite your story. *You are worth so much more.*

No matter your history, what you have done or how you see yourself, you do not deserve to be verbally abused simply because you exist. Your existence is all the proof you need that you are deserving of love, support, safety, and respect. We hope you will find inspiration in how Kendall Ann found her voice amidst the emotional despair created by her abuser. Like so many other abusive and controlling relationships, her journey towards freedom took time to unfold.

What I Know Now

1.Sticks and stones can break your bones and words can hurt your brain.

Years later, I can only remember some of the horrible words my abuser said to me, but I vividly remember the way those words made me feel. I now know this is because those words impacted my brain as significantly as the violence I would begin to endure. I am still working to repair the damage those feelings had on my self-esteem and my sense of self. Being constantly berated, insulted, and cursed at made me feel like I wasn't worthy of love, not even the love I should have had for myself. Each cruel word was not just changing the way I viewed myself, it was also changing my brain. Soon my own inner monologue began to mirror the nasty words he used against me and I started to use those words against myself. As I looked in the mirror, I didn't see someone with a healthy body; I saw someone who was "fat" and needed to lose weight, buy better clothes, and change her accent.

2. Calm your body, calm your mind.

I freely admit that I can run hot when I am angry. My face gets red, my shoulders tense up, and my teeth clench. It seems so obvious that an intense emotion like anger would affect the human body in such a profound way, but I'd never made the connection before. It makes sense that focusing on my body to impact the physical manifestations of anger would help to reel in the emotion itself. Such a realization would certainly have been more effective than the pitiful advice I received from some poor fools who have suggested I needed to "calm down" when I have been angry with them. It's comforting to know there are tasks as simple as jumping jacks, controlled breathing, and splashing water on my face that can help deescalate intense emotion.

3. Abusers use the silent treatment to punish and control their victims.

Many times when I disagreed with my abuser, he would stonewall and refuse to speak to me. He would not tell me that he was upset and needed space to think or calm down; he would simply stop interacting with me. This usually occurred if I tried to stand up for myself when he said or did something hurtful. Sometimes he would not interact with me for days, making me feel angry and worthless. So, I would have an outburst to feel heard and valued. My abuser called me "crazy" or a host of other names but never took responsibility for the way he was treating me. He would say I was the one who had the problem communicating or I couldn't control my emotions, knowing full well it was his behavior that had upset me. When I wouldn't engage during a stonewalling episode, he accused me of cheating or not caring about him because I wasn't checking in with him. To avoid stonewalling, I quit communicating my feelings about the things he did. It was another method he used to gain control of my behavior. Now I recognize how abusers can use the silent treatment as a manipulation tactic.

What Do You Know Now?

*This section is intended for you to convey your thoughts,
feelings and reflections on what you learned in the chapter by writing
or using other creative forms of expression.*

Chapter 5

Sexual Abuse

The first section of this chapter contains explicit material involving sexual abuse. If you do not feel safe or comfortable reading such material, we recommend moving onto the second part of this chapter by Dr. Kelley outlining how sexual abuse affects the survivor

The early stages of the relationship with my abuser were marked with a lot of fun and intimate sex. As with most new relationships, we had sex frequently. I figured things would simmer down once the "new love" glow wore off.

"I'm so glad you can keep up with me," my abuser mentioned once as he lay with his head on his pillow next to mine.

"What do you mean?" I asked.

"Some women just don't want to have sex as much as I do, and that really doesn't work for me." He got up from the bed and walked toward the bathroom. "Hopefully, that won't be the case with you."

I smiled cautiously and thought it was a strange thing to say but I shrugged it off as male machismo.

For nearly a year, we had what I thought was a healthy sex life, but things slowly started to change. He refused to engage in what I considered to be normal, loving affection without making it sexual. When we embraced after coming home from work, he would move his hands along my breasts or reach his hand between my legs, initiating sex. Not knowing how to assert my boundaries, I made excuses about needing to go into another room. I wanted to stop him from touching me

71

so aggressively.

After one particularly difficult day of work, I walked over to him and asked for a hug. After briefly comforting me, he slid his hand under my skirt. Immediately, I recoiled.

"Can you please not do that?" I asked.

"Not do what?" he responded.

"I want to hug you without you molesting me," I said. I tried to lighten the tone with a laugh.

"Don't you want your fiancé to be attracted to you?" he asked.

"You used to like when I touched you." He stormed out of the room and didn't speak to me for the rest of the evening.

I sat in bed that night and admonished myself. *Of course I want my fiancé to be attracted to me; maybe I overreacted. What did he really do wrong?*

I told myself that guys were just horny and not great at taking cues about affection. I reprimanded myself. Maybe he needed me to be more communicative about what type of affection I wanted. I went to bed that night committed to doing a better job of letting him know when I wanted sexual versus casual affection.

The next day I came home from work to find him in the kitchen. I paused.

"How was your day?" he asked. He hugged me and kissed me on the cheek.

"Good," I mumbled while holding my workbag and purse between us to protect my body.

He gave me a sweet kiss on my lips and broke our embrace to sit at the kitchen table.

"What do you feel like eating for dinner?" he asked. His tone was casual.

That was it. No unwanted advances. No pawing at my privates. Relief rushed through me. I figured the day before had been an anomaly and he realized how poorly he'd acted. It made me feel happy and safe.

The good behavior did not last. Within a week we were having heated arguments about my discomfort with his constant fondling. It soon became clear that the only way to stop his behavior was to avoid giving him the opportunity to touch me at all. I stopped greeting him with a hug or kiss when I came home at the end of the workday. My new scheme did not go unnoticed – or unaddressed.

"I guess you're cheating on me," he blurted out one evening.

I laughed at the absurdity of his comment. "What?"

"Since you don't even let me hug you, I know you're cheating. Everyone agrees," he said.

That pissed me off. "Does everyone know that I can't hug you without you grabbing my privates?" I asked.

"Stop accusing me of molesting you," he thundered. "I am sick of hearing about how you don't want me to touch you."

"And I am sick of having to tell you not to grab my breasts and my vagina. I want to be able to hug my fiance and feel comforted and not attacked."

He walked out of the kitchen and left me staring at my reflection in the window above the sink. *Am I really arguing with my fiancé about hugging? What is happening to me? Why can't he just touch me the way I want? Shouldn't he want to make me happy?*

He walked back into the kitchen.

"I'm sorry," he said bashfully. "I'm just so attracted to you. I always want to have sex with you because you're so hot! I'll try to do better."

He walked over to me and hugged me tightly. I was hopeful that he truly understood how upset he had made me and would alter his behavior. Still, throughout the remainder of our relationship, every time he hugged me I felt my body tighten, ready to defend myself from any unwanted advance.

I was never safe from his sexual initiations, particularly in the morning. He performed the same ritual every morning. He woke up, rolled over, and hugged me while pushing his erect penis into my back. Usually he would say something like, "Someone is excited to see you," and initiate sex. When it began, I thought it was funny. Even if I weren't totally in the mood to have sex, I would do it. The ritual grew old very quickly. Pretty soon, when he rolled over, I rebuked his advances.

He changed his strategy. He started the same – with his penis shoved into my back, but then he started kissing my neck and turning me over to kiss my breasts. Many times I made excuses for why we couldn't have sex, but sometimes I gave in just to get it over with.

One morning, I heard him stir and braced myself to feel him on my back. But, he did something unexpected. He pulled my pajama pants down. When I tried to tell him to leave me alone, he inserted his fingers into my vagina. I froze in shock, stunned by the violation of the unconsented advance. I was so surprised by his brazenness that I didn't move. I lay motionless while he kissed my neck. His fingers were still inside of me. Suddenly I snapped back to reality. "Stop!" I yelled and jumped from the bed.

"What the fuck is wrong with you?" he screamed.

"You know what is wrong with me," I said.

"You like when I do that," he said, obviously irritated.

"Don't assume I want to have sex. I want you to make sure I want to before you start." As soon as the words left my mouth, I knew we were going to have a fight.

"So, every time I want to have sex with you, I have to beg you?"

He rolled his eyes.

"You have to make sure I want it."

He jumped from the bed and walked into the bathroom. "Fucking prude."

Every evening from then on I asked him what time he needed to be up the next day and then I set my alarm fifteen minutes earlier than the time he stated to make sure I was out of bed before he woke up. On weekends, I did my best to fall asleep on the couch "accidentally" where I could wake up alone, safe from his advances.

Our fights about sex became a daily occurrence. Each time I said I didn't want to do it he either became angry or acted wounded. I never knew which would happen. Sometimes, I simply gave in and had sex to avoid his bullying. During those times I tried to imagine I was in a different place doing something else. I tried to disconnect from my body, from the despondence and shame I was feeling for giving in to sex to avoid his vitriol. Each time it happened, I felt like I lost a piece of myself.

He became more and more aggressive during intercourse, strangling me and calling me names like "slut," "bitch," and "whore." On more than one occasion, I asked him not to say those things. His response? "Oh come on. You know you like it."

Sex became something I hated. His touch scared me. I started to reject affection from everyone. I even flinched when family and friends

74

tried to hug me. I began to feel like my body was no longer my own. I had lost the power to control when and where my abuser touched me. My most important boundary was constantly being violated.

When we were in public, he'd shamelessly flirt with other women in front of me and comment, "She's hot. I'm going to ask if she wants to have a threesome" knowing I'd never do such a thing. His actions infuriated and embarrassed me. He went out of his way to interact with women to stoke my anger. When I confronted his behavior, he always told me that if I would have more sex, more adventurous sex, better sex in general, he would stop. I could change his behavior by complying to his demands. His behavior was my fault.

The stress of our tumultuous relationship caused me to feel run down. I got sick regularly. Migraine headaches, which had previously been infrequent, became consistent and I was always battling a cold. I got no reprieve from his sexual demands even when I was sick. In fact, it seemed the more physically vulnerable I was, the more he would harass me about wanting sex. I begged him to leave me alone when I was sick only to be accused of faking or exaggerating illnesses. I was a "horrible partner" even when my illnesses were obvious. I started to hide in the bathroom when I was ill just to get some peace.

"Why don't you want me to touch you?" he asked one evening as we ate dinner.

"You know why," I answered without looking up.

For half an hour he begged for my forgiveness and promised to change. He said he didn't grasp how upset he was making me feel and vowed to be a better partner and a better man. For about a month the aggressive sexual advances stopped and anytime I rejected sex, he handled it with kindness. I could tell he was trying to be a better man.

All too quickly I learned he had not changed at all. Soon, he was back to molesting me during casual affection and bullying me into having sex.

One Sunday morning I got up early to shower and to get ready to meet my cousin for brunch. It had been months since I had seen her, and I was excited. "You look great," he said to me as I fastened my necklace.

"Thank you," I replied.

"Come over here and fuck me before you leave," he said with a grunt.

"What?"

75

"What?"

"You heard me. If you're going to hang out with your cousin, you need to fuck me."

"No," I shouted. I looked in the mirror, my face was red with anger.

"That's fine; I'll just cheat on you," he said.

I was shocked. Of all the things he'd done and said to me, this was too much. He knew I would not stand for infidelity – it was a line in the sand. I looked down at my left hand. After a moment, I took off my engagement ring and placed it on bureau under the mirror.

"If you're going to threaten that, I don't want to marry you," I said, and I walked out of the house to meet my cousin.

Consent

Kendall Ann's abuser did not ask for consent. Instead he manipulated and guilted Kendall Ann into submission. If someone is forced to comply it is not consent. He took his abuse further by forcing himself on her and ignoring her requests for physical safety and agency. He used his relationship status as her fiancé as an excuse for his behavior. She did not deserve such abuse, and neither do you.

A 2019 episode of *Grey's Anatomy* focused on sexual assault and consent. The episode featured an assault survivor going through the horrors of a rape kit, and the challenge of sharing sexual trauma stories in hopes of attaining justice. The episode was inspired by Christine Blasley Ford's 2018 testimony where she accused Justice Brett Kavanaugh of sexually assaulting her in the summer of 1982.

Her testimony did not bring Christine Blasley the justice she deserved. At the time of the hearing, clients I was working with who had experienced sexual abuse in the past relayed that the confirmation hearing was highly triggering for them. Despite the evidence, Blasey's story did not block Kavanaugh's confirmation to the Supreme Court. Once again, a survivor was silenced and the abuser advanced. The injustice Christine Blasley faced in the outcome of the hearing further affirmed the need for change regarding sexual abuse, power dynamics, and sexism as a whole. The *Grey's Anatomy* episode featured an excellent example of simple, but essential changes we can institute to educate our children about consent.

The plot of the episode followed a male character and his son going out to a diner for a meal. The son thought it was just a casual outing, but the father wanted to focus on the topic of consent with his son, a teen, who had just started dating. Addressing the potentially uncomfortable topic head-on, the father said, "If at any point she is not enjoying herself, you stop. Time out. No matter what."

The scene was important because it highlighted a topic in our media and in society that had been ignored, though it certainly should not have been. The "birds and the bees" talk has long been a rite of passage for many young boys and girls. The conversation is usually convened by parents, care givers, or even educators, and it traditionally explores the nuances of relationships, such as what it means to "date" someone, the mechanics of sexual intercourse, and the potential dangers of pregnancy and sexually transmitted diseases. Unfortunately, the "talk" has not historically highlighted the concept of consent. Teaching young children that they have the right to agree or disagree to any and all forms of physical intimacy at any and all times is imperative. Consent is clear. If it is not clear, it does not qualify.

For example, if someone is too intoxicated to agree to any form of physical intimacy, yet they are not lucid enough to say "no," *this is* **not** *consent.* The conversation concerning consent should be just as important as the conversation about STDs. It is extremely **sexy** to allow choice. "Boys will be boys" is **not sexy at all**.

The Me Too movement highlights the harmful messaging regarding consent in the male-female relationship, something that begins as early as the neighborhood sandbox. The classic and unfortunate narrative tells a young girl that if a boy is picking on her, it must be because he **likes** her. Such thinking is dangerous, illogical, and irresponsible. It should never be permissible to treat someone poorly due to frustration, nervousness, or insecurity. Dismissing a lack of respect as "natural youthful behavior" sets the stage for an imbalance of power or worse. Flirting, something natural and perhaps inevitable, should never deteriorate into a form of torture. Let's do better in teaching our children how to treat each other.

Consent is defined as "permission for something to happen or agreement to do something." But what if someone changes their mind? A website dedicated to the idea of consent, www.consentnation.com, takes the term a step farther and shares a definition that offers a broader understanding of what consent should look like by using the FRIES acronym.

Consent is...

1. Freely Given: A person says yes without the application of threats, pressure, force, and/or coercion. Consent can't be given if the person is under the influence of alcohol or drugs, and/or passed out.

2. Reversible: You can say yes and then change your mind at any point.

3. Informed: Consent can only happen if the person has an honest understanding of the situation. (Example: If someone says he's going to use a condom and doesn't, there is no consent)

4. Enthusiastic: Consent is clear, such as an excited yes! You should never feel like you're expected to do anything.

5. Specific: Saying yes to one thing (ex: making out) does not mean consent to something else (ex: sex). Consent is never implied.

Consent is freely given, reversible, informed, enthusiastic and specific. Open communication is essential in ensuring safe and consensual sex. Kendall Ann's abuser did not respect these principles and he manipulated her into thinking he would accept her right to ask for what she did or did not want. He led her to believe that he would accept when she said no to sex. He promised he would provide the intimacy she wanted, a hug or a kiss, that did not have to become something sexual or provocative. But these promises were forms of lies and manipulation.

Her abuser threatened her when it came to sex. According to him, if she loved him she would want to have sex with him no matter what. In his mind if she said "yes" once, her permission could not be reversed or retracted. He would not allow her to change her mind because she was in a committed relationship with him. Her boundaries were not her own.

The Word "Relationship" Still Comes with Boundaries

Intimate relationships form out of emotional and/or physical connection, but physical intimacy is never a requirement or expectation. At the beginning of Kendall Ann's relationship she felt comfortable with how often she and her abuser were having sex, though she did mention early thoughts about it being more frequent than she normally would prefer. Before she could voice her concern, her abuser made sure the tone was set so she could not safely express her desires. As we recall, he said things like:

"I'm so glad you can keep up with me."

"Some women just don't want to have sex as much as I do, and that really doesn't work for me."

"Hopefully, that won't be the case with you."

His words laid out a manipulative and controlling landscape since they were neither exploratory nor open-ended. They did not invite a response of her own desires.

There is an adage in couples' counseling that another person is not responsible for your happiness. Each individual is responsible for their own well-being. Ideally when you come together as a couple, you can create an even more expansive "whole" together. The opposite of a healthy and expansive perspective on dating and relationships occurs when boundaries are crossed and one or both people in a relationship begin blaming the other for how they feel. This is a sign of poor individuality in the relationship and can indicate the potential for abuse of power in the future.

Kendall Ann's abuser made many assumptions about her desires and permissions concerning her body. Sometimes he assaulted her in passive aggressive ways that made his intentions sometimes hard to read; other times he was outright aggressive, mean, and threatening. It was not always clear if he was expressing his lust for her, or if what he was doing was abusive. He clearly understood the mechanics of pushing boundaries as opposed to breaking them aggressively. When Kendall Ann asked for physical affection and closeness, such as a kiss or a hug, without sexual advancement from him, she was met with passive aggressive resistance. Her abuser challenged whether she were attracted to him, or whether she wanted him to touch her at all. He used guilt to get what he wanted when it came to sex. This should *never* be the case. Any time guilt is being used to *convince* someone to agree to sex, without freely giving consent, there is a problem with sexual coercion. *Sexual coercion* is a **Red Flag** that needs to be recognized as problematic and dangerous.

When Boundaries Break

In an intimate relationship an abuser often tends to **push** boundaries as opposed to **breaking** them, in an effort to manipulate their victim with unpredictability. *Unstable boundaries* is a **Red Flag** that was evident in Kendall Ann's relationship. When Kendall Ann finally started expressing her overt anger, her abuser met her resistance with aggression and violence, such as strangling her during sex. Then he turned the tables by trying to make her feel like it was something she wanted. He used the trust he had built and the love he promised as means for making his despicable behavior both hard to interpret and, from his perspective, acceptable.

Our bodies are sacred and should never be treated with aggression or dishonor. All acts *must* be completely and enthusiastically engaged in by both partners. There is nothing immoral about aggressive or adventurous sex as long as it is consensual. Every single time you engage in intimacy with your partner, you have the right to change your mind in any way at any time; you are the steward of your own body. One day you may want to be handled with gentle care, the next day with more dominating and animalistic expressions of desire, but that is entirely up to you *each and every time*. As mentioned, consent is always 100% reversible.

Kendall Ann's abuser knew exactly how to guilt and manipulate her into *having sex to get it over with*. Her agreement to stop his torment was not an example of consent; her compliance was not "freely given" or "enthusiastic." Instead it was capitulation to avoid negative repercussions. He attacked her resistance with threats: *"If you don't satisfy me, I will cheat on you."* Once this boundary was breeched, she reached the breaking point. She took off her engagement ring, declared he had crossed the line one too many times, and walked bravely out the door.

What I Know Now

1. Giving consent once is not a blank check.

Even if you are in a relationship and have given consent to sex before, you are not obligated to be intimate with your partner all the time. Since I had started a sexual relationship with him, my abuser felt I could never say "no." He made me feel like I was doing something wrong by not desiring sex any time he wanted it. Saying "yes" once doesn't mean you always have to consent. It is your body, and you are allowed to decide when you engage in intimacy. It doesn't matter if you are dating, engaged, or have been married for 30 years, your body belongs to you and not to your partner. You have an equal say in when you have sex.

2. I didn't realize I was being sexually abused while it was happening.

I thought my abuser's actions were my fault. Each time I got to a breaking point and confronted him about his behavior he stopped his sexual advances for a time. But he always reverted to aggression. Now I understand the manipulation. He had no interest in hearing me. He was never truly trying to change. Instead, he understood when I reached a flash point and he needed to back down for a period. Now I realize it's not okay to coerce, bully, or manipulate someone into having sex. I thought my abuser was just being a jerk, simply because I didn't fully grasp the severity of what was taking place. Some nights he would keep me awake for hours, badgering me to have sex until I complied. That is not healthy. The "boys will be boys" message our culture deems acceptable had a huge impact on me. I did not view his attacks as wrong; I thought they were the way men acted. I should have recognized his actions as dangerous and disrespectful. If you are having sex with your partner simply to keep the peace, or you dread it when your partner touches you, think about why you're feeling that way. Don't push those feelings down. They are there for a reason.

3. I should never have sex if I don't want to.

Sexual intimacy should be a safe, fun, pleasurable experience for both parties. I should never sacrifice my own happiness and sanity for my partner's sexual satisfaction. I shouldn't be in a relationship with someone who forces me to make that choice. Conceding to sexual contact when you don't want it is unhealthy and has a serious impact on your self-esteem and self-worth. Most importantly, sex should never be necessary to "keep the peace" in a relationship. If you feel uncomfortable with things your partner does during sex, you must communicate those feelings. If your concern is met with any other reaction than acceptance, reevaluate whether you should be in the relationship. You should not be with someone who doesn't respect your boundaries during something as intimate as sex.

What Do You Know Now?

This section is intended for you to convey your thoughts, feelings and reflections on what you learned in the chapter by writing or using other creative forms of expression.

Chapter 6

Physical Abuse

The first section of this chapter contains explicit material involving physical abuse. If you do not feel safe or comfortable reading such material, we recommend moving onto the second part of this chapter by Dr. Kelley outlining how physical abuse affects the survivor

Before this moment, the abuse had never been physical.

"I don't want to speak to you right now!" I yelled at my abuser.

We were deep into a typical argument and neither of us was backing down. I needed a break. I needed to breathe. I walked towards the door of the bedroom. He shifted his body to block the way.

"What are you doing?" I asked. "Let me out of the room. I need a minute away from you."

"No," he replied. He crossed his arms and centered his bulk in the opening.

I stood for a moment, confused. *What is he doing?*

"Seriously, let me out," I demanded.

His voice boomed. "You're not leaving this room until you understand why you're wrong!"

I wanted to get away. "Excuse me," I said as I tried to slide past him. The situation erupted. He stepped towards me, slammed my face and chest against the wall, and then crushed me between his body and the doorframe.

"What the fuck?" I yelled.

"You're not hurt," he roared. He grabbed my wrist and yanked me; our faces were inches apart. "Don't do that again," he threatened. He released my wrist and slung my arm like he was tossing away a soda can.

I decided to get out of the house. Confused and fearful, I grabbed my dog, Ozzy, attached his leash, and went to the state park at the end of our street. As Ozzy and I walked through the park I thought about what happened. I had a hard time organizing the whirlwind of thoughts in my head. I wasn't physically hurt, but I felt something very wrong had just happened. We'd had tension in our relationship for a while, but his body smashing me against the doorframe was something new – something dreadful – something terrifying.

I decided to confront him when I got back to the house. When I walked in, he was sitting on the couch watching tv.

"We need to talk about what just happened," I said.

"What do you mean?" he asked.

"You shoved me into the door frame, you grabbed my wrist, and you screamed in my face." I took a deep breath and tried to fight the tightness creeping into my shoulders. "Don't ever do that again," I said. My voice was flat and stern.

He looked smug.

"This is on you," he said. "I was just standing there, and you tried to get by. You knew you couldn't fit, and you bumped into me."

He spit out a dismissive laugh. Nothing I said had registered.

We had been together for over a year and we were engaged. I knew from experience that arguing with him would not help. Regardless, I was determined to speak my truth.

"That is absolutely not true," I said. I repeated my condemnation. "You pushed me into the doorframe, you grabbed my wrist, and you screamed in my face. Never, ever do that again."

He jumped up from the couch. "I didn't do shit!" I could feel his breath on me; he was less than an inch away.

My heart pounded; my breath pushed deep into my belly; I could not believe this. Terrified, I ran out of the room and locked myself in the bedroom with Ozzy. The fragile boundary separating our arguments from violence was quickly evaporating.

I sat on the bed and stared at the phone in my hand. I needed advice. I started to call my mom and stopped. If I told her the truth I feared she would hate my fiancé. I worried that a single incident could forever ruin her positive feelings about his becoming part of our family. I put the phone on the bed next to me, unsure of what to do next.

That instance of physical aggression was not a one-time thing. Soon, every argument ended in him physically blocking me in some way. In the heat of an argument, he tried to cage me in and control where and how I could move. Some days he simply stood in the doorway and yelled in my face; his hot breath blew against the tears dripping down my cheeks. Other times, if I tried to walk away, he grabbed my arm or wrist. I felt the relationship's temperature rising. The only thing I could do to stop him from being aggressive was not to engage in any arguments. I began agreeing with almost anything he said just to avoid a physical altercation.

My behavior did not satisfy him. He grew meaner and crueler. One evening as I worked on my laptop in our guest bedroom, I heard his footsteps coming down the hallway. I straightened my spine and readied myself for whatever was about to happen.

"Do you plan on giving me any fucking attention tonight or are you just going to sit in here on your computer?" His voice was loud and accusatory.

"I'm working," I said. I never looked up from my screen.

"Turn around and look at me," he screamed. "Stop ignoring me."

"Please leave me alone," I begged. "I'm trying to do a little extra work."

"You're such a selfish bitch," he bellowed.

I stood and walked toward the door.

"I want to get away from you." My voice was a low growl. "Get out of my way."

He grabbed my shoulders and shoved me to the ground. My head hit the chair where I had just been sitting.

He lurched toward me. "You will never tell me what to do!" He was less than a hand width from my face, screaming. He turned and walked out.

I curled into the fetal position, crying and shaking. Ozzy cuddled up next to me and I wept into his fur. To this point my abuser had intimidated and bullied, but I never dreamed he would become violent, that he would shove me.

87

What I Wish I Knew

Am I being abused? Is this how it starts?

I needed help. I didn't leave the room that night. I researched resources on abuse for hours. I was so confused. I lay in bed and cried all night, fearful of what could happen the next day.

When I emerged from the room in the morning, my abuser was in the kitchen. Fear hit me like a lightning bolt; all my muscles reflexively tensed.

"Good Morning, Beautiful," he said with a smile. He grabbed his bag and headed for the door. "Have a great day!"

My knees shook as I sat down at the kitchen table. *Where is the apology for pushing me? For screaming at me? Where is the acknowledgement that something very wrong took place? What is happening to my life?*

I reassessed. I'd spent all night doing research on the internet about abuse. Now, according to my abuser, everything was okay? Was he even going to address what he had done? What was going to happen to us? What was going to happen to me? Was I going to be okay? Was there even something wrong?

That afternoon when he came home, he had miraculously transformed back into the man I fell in love with. There was no shouting, name calling, or aggressive posturing for several weeks. I figured he understood the gravity of what he had done and was too embarrassed to bring it up. To help let it go, I chose to assume he was probably very sorry and ashamed. We were going to be okay.

I let down my guard.

When I was in my mid-twenties, my parents had been very generous and given me some money for my wedding. I had invested it in hopes that I would fall in love one day and use it to help fund a beautiful ceremony and a great party. My abuser and I had planned a small destination wedding. Soon after, I was taking money from my investments to pay for our flights, a boat outing for our guests the day before the wedding, the cake, a reservation at a lovely restaurant for our reception, a car rental, and a villa where we would stay for several days before and after our nuptials. My abuser didn't offer to pay a penny. Although I was a little troubled by this, I figured the parents of the bride traditionally paid for the wedding, so I didn't dwell on his lack of support.

My abuser's stepfather decided not to attend our island wedding. Without consulting me, my abuser invited his mother to stay in our villa.

I didn't have anything against his mother, but having my soon-to-be mother-in-law stay with us during our romantic wedding trip wasn't what I had in mind.

When I voiced my reservations, he became enraged and yelled about what a "selfish bitch" I was. I told him that if she wanted to stay in the villa I was paying for, she'd need to pay a portion of the bill. Both my parents and his father were paying for their housing; why should I pay for his mother's? The argument continued for days.

One night his father and stepmother invited us out for dinner. We drank several glasses of wine and talked about how excited we were for the upcoming wedding. When we arrived home, I poured myself a glass of wine and changed into my pajamas. Feeling brave because of the wine, I decided I would revisit the mother-in-law issue with my fiancé. I asked him to tell his mother that she'd have to contribute to the villa or find somewhere else to stay. It did not go well. He followed me from room to room. He told me what a horrible person I was, saying he probably shouldn't marry someone that was "selfish," "disgusting," "fat," and a "bitch."

I walked into the guestroom and opened my laptop to check my email. He followed me in and slammed the laptop closed.

"Leave me alone!" I screamed as loudly as possible hoping to get him out of the room.

He stood in the center of the room and shouted about how horrible I was. I knew I had to leave. When I moved to get out of the room, he squared himself in the center of the door once again.

"Get out of my way. I don't want to be around you!" I yelled. I stepped forward. Like before, he pushed me hard, but this time I stayed on my feet. Anger seeped out of every pore in my body. Impulsively, I picked up my glass and threw wine in his face hoping it would disarm him and get him out of my way.

The next thing I knew I was lying on my back and struggling to breathe. His hands were wrapped around my neck. I gasped for air. I tried pulling his hands from my neck, but I could not dislodge them.

He's choking me. Oh my God, he's choking me.

Suddenly, I could breathe again. He had jumped off of me, stormed out of the room, and slammed the door. I ran to the bathroom, gasping for air. I looked in the mirror and saw two red handprints materializing on my throat.

Something in me snapped. I stomped into the living room. He was sitting on the couch. I began to howl. "You're going to jail. Look what you did to me."

"You can't prove I did that," he snarled. "You did it to yourself."

In that moment, all hope I had that he had changed for the better evaporated. He was violent, and it was escalating. The reality of the situation finally hit me. *This is very, very bad.* I raced back into the guest room and locked the door behind me. I heard his footsteps following me. Without hesitation I picked up my phone and dialed 911. I explained to the operator what happened. I knew my fiancé was listening through the door. I heard him walk out of the house, start his car, and drive away.

Fearful he would return before the police got there, I took the phone onto the front porch and sat on the stairs with Ozzy, my protector. The operator stayed on the line until two officers arrived. They assessed the situation and took notes as I explained what happened. The details poured from my soul. I told them everything from how he had evolved from shouting and sometimes blocking me in rooms to shoving me to the ground and strangling me. It didn't feel real. I was baring my soul to two strangers. They now knew things even my mother didn't know. I wanted help. I needed someone to help me be safe.

The officers noted everything I said and took pictures of the hand prints on my neck.

"We need to call an ambulance," one of the officers said to me. He had a kind voice. "This is very serious, and you need to be seen by a doctor."

I froze. An ambulance? The hospital? What was I doing? I was about to marry this man; I could not send him to jail. How could I be so selfish? I loved him and now he'd be ruined because of a single mistake.

I sat on the curb and sobbed. My voice cracked. "I can't," I said, "I can't do this."

The officers gave each other a knowing glance. "Miss, you really need to think about what went on tonight. The man you live with strangled you."

"I can't do this," I repeated. I was torn. I knew what he had done was wrong, unacceptable, unforgivable, and yet I could not be the *reason* he got in trouble.

"Miss," said the other, less patient officer, "these things never get better. They only get worse. He could have killed you. Look at your neck."

"I can't do this," I sobbed. It was the only sentence I could find. The only words I could get out. I couldn't say he didn't do it, because he did, but I couldn't admit what he did for fear of what it would set into motion. I was paralyzed.

The officers handed me a card with a case number on it and the phone number of the detective who would be assigned to my case.

The kinder officer looked me in the eyes. "Please be careful." They left.

I walked back into the house and took pictures of my neck. I sent them to a trustworthy co-worker that I knew my abuser wouldn't be able to locate. I barricaded myself into the guest bedroom in case my abuser returned home and tried to open the door. For the rest of the night, I held Ozzy and sobbed while wishing I could somehow erase the whole evening. Later, I heard my abuser come into the house and I held my breath. I hoped he wouldn't try to find me. Luckily, he didn't. I didn't know how I'd get through the night without losing my mind or dying of heartache. I had entered a new world, a scary place I knew nothing about. I was afraid I wouldn't live to see my wedding.

The next morning I gathered all of my strength and walked down the hall as quietly as I could. My abuser was sitting on the couch in the living room, waiting.

"Congratulations on ruining my fucking life," he whispered as I walked into the room. "I really hope you didn't tell them you wanted to press charges, because if you did, I can't marry you."

I stood without saying anything as a tidal wave of confusion crashed over me. *He strangled me – how is it now something that I did wrong?* I looked at the floor and he started screaming about how I had ruined his career, his life, and his reputation.

"Fix it," he demanded. "Call the detective and tell him you don't want to press charges," he roared. He stomped out the house slamming the door behind him so violently that it shook the windows.

I dragged myself into the bathroom, weary from the stress. I splashed cold water on my face and stared into the mirror. I didn't recognize the woman staring back at me. It was as if I had been replaced by someone else. My eyes were barely open, swollen and red from a night of weeping. I leaned closer to get a better look at my neck. I could still make out the red marks from his fingers. What was I supposed to do? I wished there were someone I could call and talk to, someone who would tell me the right choice to make.

I went back into the office and sat in my desk chair for what seemed like hours and fiddled with the card the police had given me. I was conflicted. I didn't want to save my abuser from punishment, but I also didn't want him to be in trouble. He was my fiancé, the person I was going to spend my life with. How could I send him to jail for one mistake? Maybe it was my fault for throwing the wine at him. If I had not done that, he wouldn't have strangled me.

Strangled. The word hung heavily in my mind. My fiancé had strangled me. What would I tell any other woman in my position? I'd tell her to leave. I'd tell her, "Gather your shit, leave that house, and never ever return." The thought of doing that made me nauseated.

I love him. It was one mistake. One bad night.

But it wasn't. How many times had I been pushed into a door jamb? Shoved to the ground? Screamed at? Now strangled? How many more violent moments would there be?

Strangled. I kept coming back to that word. The word I'd heard on the news and in crime shows. What did it mean? Being strangled seemed so serious when I thought about it happening to other people. Now, it had happened to me.

Was it as equally as serious now?

I pictured him in jail, separated from everything he loved, his life in shambles. What would he do when he got out? How would be get a job? How would he take care of himself? It would be my fault because I put him there. How could I live with myself after ruining someone's life?

I reached for my phone. I dialed the phone number on the card. The moment of truth. When the other side picked up on the first ring, I hesitated. I timidly gave my name and my case number and told the detective I did not want to press charges.

The detective said my call would be taken into consideration and if this were my fiancé's first offense, charges probably wouldn't be pressed. Before hanging up he asked one last time if I were sure. I paused. I wasn't sure, but I also wasn't ready to give up on the man I loved. I answered "yes" and hung up.

Then, I lowered my head to the desk in front of me and sobbed.

Blame and Violence

Up to this point, Kendall Ann had endured multiple forms of painful verbal and emotional abuse. The manipulation, silence, gaslighting, and intimidation were certainly enough to end a relationship, but when her abuser shoved his weight against her to intimidate, control, and inflict harm, something snapped. Instead of someone who would protect her from physical harm, he was someone from whom she needed to be protected.

Still, Kendall Ann struggled with internalizing blame, something familiar to many survivors of abuse. This is a common cognitive distortion connected to abuse and assault. Many survivors believe they could have done something to prevent the behavior, or that they are somehow to blame for the actions of their abuser. Kendall Ann's thoughts were flooded by cognitive distortions: *I knew what he had done was wrong, unacceptable, unforgivable, and yet I could not go through with being the <u>reason</u> he got in trouble for it.*

Displacement of blame becomes a major psychological sticking point regarding when and how someone finally leaves an abusive relationship. Many abusers have issues with authority and seek to control others. They often do not take the blame for their misdeeds. Instead, they blame others for their own poor choices.

Kendall Ann should not have felt any form of guilt for the consequences her abuser would have to suffer. **He** put his hands on her; **he** threatened her; **he** intimidated her. Looking back at the inception of their relationship, when the emotional abuse started, it was apparent that the displacement of blame. There is no excuse or justification for physically harming another person, especially a romantic partner. No level of frustration, sorrow, betrayal, or emotional tension permits physical violence and intimidation, **period**. Tolerating violence at any level can only lead to exceedingly more dangerous outcomes.

Dangers of Strangulation

One of the most dangerous forms of physical violence is strangulation, defined as *the obstruction of blood vessels and or airflow in the neck resulting in asphyxia.* There is no gray area with strangulation. Any act of

Any act of *strangulation* is a **Red Flag** and a sign of potential, serious harm. There must be a **zero-tolerance** policy regarding strangulation and intimate partner violence. Strangulation is an active alarm that something horrible is happening. There is no way for someone to be *strangled just a little bit.* It either is strangulation, or it isn't, black or white. Do not allow an abuser to minimize the danger or intent of such an action.

All instances of strangulation, or being choked, can lead to permanent damage to the throat and brain through brain cell death which is rapid and often fatal. Of the one in four women who will suffer intimate partner violence (IVP), 68% of those will experience near fatal strangulation (www.StrangulationTrainingInstitute.com). Do not take this statistic lightly. **If you have been choked by your partner before, you are far more likely to be choked again.** The risk of serious injury and death from strangulation are far too great to ignore.

If you have been strangled, please understand that the danger is not over; death or serious injury can occur days after the attack. Strangulation can lead to carotid artery dissection and complications such as pneumonia, acute respiratory distress syndrome (ARDS), and/or the risk of blood clots traveling to the brain (embolization). If you experience this form of abuse, please contact your local medical provider immediately. For more help and information, call the National Domestic Violence Hotline at 800-799-7233 (SAFE) or visit www.StrangulationTrainingInstitute.com.

The Effects of Violence on Body and Mind

The impact physical violence has on the body and mind is incredibly complex and varied. No matter the degree, any form of abuse is an invasion of your sacred and personal space. You have the right to feel safe in your own skin. When experiencing danger or a threat of harm from an abuser, there is a myriad of protective reactions your brain carries out to keep you from becoming overwhelmed from the trauma of violence. Post-traumatic stress disorder (PTSD) is a natural phenomenon designed to help keep you alive. Hypervigilance to your environment is a survival skill. *Hypervigilance* is the elevated state of constantly assessing potential threats around you and often a result of trauma. Unfortunately, long-term side effects of severe stress from abuse can also lead to; depression, suicidal ideation, memory problems, nightmares, anxiety, amnesia, and psychosis. We will explore these mechanisms closer in **Chapter 8: The Aftermath.**

Healing The Body From Violence

Healing the physical effects of trauma have been thoughtfully and extensively explored by Boston-based Dutch psychiatrist and pioneering PTSD researcher, Bessel Van De Kolk, in his 2014 book, *The Body Keeps the Score*. If you have experienced any form of trauma in your past, or are currently enduring the trauma of abuse, this book offers significant insight.

Historically it was believed that trauma could be addressed simply by talking about it. Retelling the trauma story was believed to bring insight and resolution necessary to heal and move forward. The hope is that clients will gain insight by working with a supportive therapist and will gain greater self-esteem, more effective thinking strategies, and an increased ability to manage intense emotions.

This approach has been proven to provide many benefits and if you do not have a therapist, you can also choose to talk to a trusted, supportive person. There is one issue to consider however with relying solely on the cognitive process of retelling a trauma story, which is that the process of retelling can be triggering to some survivors. This is why other creative forms of expression can sometimes feel safer and more effective. Some examples include; art therapy, dance and movement therapy, writing, music therapy, EMDR and Accelerated Resolution Therapy. All of these forms of therapy rely on expression of emotion and sensations without the need to retell details of trauma. This can be helpful because trauma does not get stored as a linear memory with a beginning, middle, and end. Instead it manifests as a "felt sense" in the body full of imagery, sensations, and beliefs.

In addition to the negative impact that abuse can have on the "felt sense" of the body, there are a number of ways emotional and physical abuse alter the way your brain and body and function. These include:

- Changes to the prefrontal cortex (responsible for regulating emotional responses). Changes may inhibit the ability to regulate the emotions necessary for leaving your abuser
- Night terrors and insomnia, which lead to fatigue and difficulty in concentrating
- Agitation and anxiety especially in unfamiliar places

- An extreme startle reflex, which can result in rage, further withdrawal from social situations, or personal relationships
- Anger, rage, and mood swings
- Feelings of numbness or being otherwise disconnected from reality and those around you
- Inexplicable aches and pains
- Racing heart, high blood pressure, and difficulty controlling blood sugar levels
- Chronic health conditions related to stress

After acute trauma it is common to experience some of the psychological and physiological symptoms previously listed. For example, after a car accident most people will have experiences of a racing heart or extreme startle reflex when they get into a car. This does not mean the person has developed PTSD if these symptoms present within the first few weeks after a trauma. If however the symptoms persist it can be beneficial to assess for PTSD. According to *USA's Mental Health First Aid©*, there are specific ways to determine if your trauma response is escalating towards the early development of PTSD, or a chronic stress disorder.

- You cannot stop thinking about the trauma
- You remain upset or fearful
- You are unable to escape intense, ongoing, distressing feelings
- You find important relationships are suffering
- You feel jumpy
- You have nightmares related to trauma
- You are unable to enjoy life as a result of the trauma
- You have symptoms that are interfering with usual activities

It is recommended to seek out professional help if these symptoms are present for **four weeks or more** after the trauma event.

Believe in Your Experience

If you have experienced physical assault or violence, or if you

96

Believe in Your Experience

If you have experienced physical assault or violence, or if you understand your relationship is heading in that direction, validate yourself **now**. Kendall Ann's story shows how important this is. So many times in her relationship she felt *confused* by what was happening. Her intuition was offering her a warning she was not yet ready to hear.

Sometimes, listening to your inner voice is difficult, especially if your abusive relationship has caused *cognitive dissonance*. Cognitive dissonance causes you to hold more than one type of belief at any given time that contradict your beliefs, values, or ideas.

For example: you are in an abusive relationship and you strongly believe violence is wrong and that women should have a voice and be able to express themselves. But because of cognitive dissonance, you may overlook some of your beliefs to preserve what is left of your relationship. Trusting your true self and intuition may feel impossible at times, but it is the underlying message of this book.

- Listen to your intuition, not to the lies you were told
- You are worthy of safety and your feelings are valid
- Taking the blame for your abuser's actions has to stop now
- Whether it is the police, a trusted friend, a family member, or a therapist, your story is valid, and it deserves to be told

To trust your inner voice and break out of cognitive dissonance, you must believe in your own story. Kendall Ann struggled to believe hers when she had to commit to pressing charges. The police urged her to follow through, but a part of her held her back and made it hard to gauge the level of her potential danger. She looked for answers on the internet and she summoned support from law enforcement. Still, she could not fully commit.

We want to offer you a space here to reflect on what has happened in your relationship up to this point. Perhaps asking yourself what led you to pick up this book in the first place. We hope these guiding questions will encourage you to believe in your story, and to pause and listen to the voice of your intuition. If you feel unsafe for any reason writing your your answers in this book, you can still benefit from mental reflection, which can be equally as powerful. Putting a date on what you write may also aid you in the future if you choose to take any legal action. (We will explore legal advice for leaving and safety in the next chapter).

For now, take a moment and be still. Gently allow space in your mind. Take a deep breath, pause, exhale, and use the powerful, therapeutic tool of writing to explore your own story.

My Story

Date of Entry:_____

1. Do I now feel (or have I ever felt) unsafe with my partner? If so, what has my partner done to make me feel this way?

2. How would I describe my sense of safety in my present relationship and what do I most believe about this relationship?

3. If outsiders looked at my relationship, what would they see?

4. If I were to share these truths with someone, who would it be and what might I tell them? (Rehearsing or writing out what you wish to share can reduce anxiety and increase the likelihood of following through with your plan).

A Moment For Self-Care

Any time I close an intense trauma session with a client, I always encourage them to take time to do three specific things for themselves by the end of the day. After reflecting on some difficult aspects of your relationship, I would encourage you to do the same. You deserve it.

1. If you need to cry, cry. If you need to scream, go for it. If you need to shake and move your body, listen to your body and get moving. Give yourself the release you need, for as long as you need it. If you do not have a private space, park your car and let it all out in solitude.

2. If you need to talk, reach out to someone as soon as you can. Even if you do not tell them specifics, the simple act of talking with another person can provide healthy self-regulation.

3. Do something kind for yourself, something that relaxes you. (Ex. Exercise, yoga, painting, a bath, cooking, or even taking a much-needed nap as sleep helps us process our thoughts and emotions).

What I Know Now

1. Strangulation is more dangerous than I thought.

Before I left my abuser and told my story, I had no idea what the implications of strangulation were. I thought it was a dangerous, scary act that needed to be taken seriously, but I didn't know the lasting physical effects it could have. I also wasn't aware how grave the statistics on strangulation are. I now understand the magnitude of the danger; the act should not be ignored or downplayed. Choking, strangulation, or any variant of these acts can lead to death. Even if the police had explained the facts to me, I am not sure I would have truly heard what they were saying. I also understand how lucky I am that my abuser didn't kill me or cause serious harm to my body when he was strangling me. It could have easily happened.

2. It is not my fault.

This lesson has taken me longer to accept than I'd like to admit. My abuser had programmed me through gaslighting to take responsibility for everything wrong in our relationship; it became natural for me to take the blame for his abuse. As with all of his previous, horrible behavior, I felt as though I had done something to bring it upon myself and that I could fix it by knowing and doing better. Not true. If someone makes the choice to use violence against you, they are responsible. I now understand there is never any reason for someone to push me into a door jamb, push me to the floor, grab parts of my body aggressively, or strangle me. These were his actions, and he is the only one responsible for them.

3. It's difficult to choose what to do when your brain, heart, and gut are sending you different messages.

When you love someone and are being brainwashed by them, you can rationalize nearly everything they do, but your gut can't. If you're feeling confused about your partner's actions, it's probably because your gut and your brain are at war. Your gut is trying to keep you safe. Listen to it. Trust it. There is no reason your partner should ever be violent towards you. If your partner is using violence to punish or control you, you are in serious danger and you need to take the necessary steps to protect yourself. My heart wanted to believe that my abuser didn't mean to hurt me because I loved him so deeply. This allowed me to excuse dangerous behavior. Making the choice whether to press charges against him was one of the most difficult decisions I ever faced. I blamed myself for his violence. When I thought he might be punished, the guilt was unbearable. Now I know my guilt was misdirected. He deserved any and all consequences as a result of his conscious choice to strangle me.

What Do You Know Now?

*This section is intended for you to convey your thoughts,
feelings and reflections on what you learned in the chapter by writing
or using other creative forms of expression.*

Chapter 7

Leaving

"The most difficult steps of recovery and change are the first ones."

The first section of this chapter contains explicit material involving physical abuse. If you do not feel safe or comfortable reading such material, we recommend moving onto the second part of this chapter by Dr. Kelley outlining how to get out safely

Although I didn't press charges on my abuser, something in me changed that day. My body was heavy, and my brain was cloudy. I felt like I could burst into tears at any moment. My abuser acted as though nothing had happened. In fact, only days after I called the police, he began sexually abusing and bullying me again.

He exhibited a deep rage; I was lucky to escape his strangling me without serious injury or worse. But still, I stayed hoping something would change. It wasn't until the morning I was going to meet my cousin for brunch, the same morning he'd threatened to sleep with someone else if I would not have sex with him, that I decided I would leave for good. It was the last instance of disrespect I could tolerate; he had hit the trip wire. As an outward symbol of my internal disgust, I removed my ring and never wore it again.

When I walked into the restaurant to meet my cousin, my stomach churned. I thought I was going to be sick. Somehow the restaurant felt brighter and sounded louder than when I had been there previously. I collapsed into a chair across from Christine and took a deep breath. Before we even put in our orders, I told her everything. Every detail. The name calling. The sexual bullying. The violence. I saw the heartbreak in her eyes as I bared my soul to her.

I told her I was leaving him. My plan was to return home and avoid him for the evening. The next morning I'd lease an apartment. Once I secured a place to live, I would move out. My cousin was worried about my safety, but I told her I'd lock myself in a room where he couldn't get to me and I wouldn't tell him I was leaving until the next day.

Even though I just returned from eating brunch with my cousin, I got back to the house to find he had made me my favorite meal. I could tell he sensed that he was losing control. I told him I wasn't hungry and took Ozzy into the bedroom where I stayed all night. Late into the evening, he knocked on the door. I held my breath and prayed he'd assume I was asleep when I didn't answer. He knocked once more, then retreated. I spent the night staring at the ceiling, terrified he would return.

The next morning, I dressed and readied myself to tell him that it was over. It did not go as planned. When I told him our engagement was off and I was leaving to secure an apartment, he didn't cry or beg me to stay. Instead, he laughed at me. The person who was supposed to be my teammate, my everything, laughed in my face when I told him I wanted to leave. Even after everything he had done to me, his laughter broke my heart.

I drove to the apartment complex where I had lived at the beginning of our relationship and through tears, explained that I needed an apartment as soon as possible. Thankfully, there was something available and I could move in immediately. Before signing the lease, I called my abuser and told him this was his last chance. His voice blasted through my earpiece. He did not care about our relationship anymore. He said I was embarrassing both of us with my behavior, but if I wanted to leave I should "fucking go." With that, I hung up and signed the lease on the table in front of me.

I had considered leaving before, but this was the farthest I had ever gotten in the process. When I lived with my abuser, but still had my old apartment, there were several times I had packed a bag, collected Ozzy, and spent the night away. Usually, my abuser begged me to return, and I did. But this time was different. This time I wouldn't be back. I was not going to be fooled by a 24-hour cooling down period and an apology that

that never manifested into changed behavior.

I went back to the house to gather my necessities; my laptop for work, toiletries, whatever clothes I could grab quickly, and most importantly, Ozzy. When I arrived and saw his car in the driveway, I did not feel a sense of alarm. I figured I would be in and out quickly. I could withstand whatever venomous words he spewed in my direction during what was sure to be a short interaction. I was ready. I never once considered that the encounter might turn violent and dangerous.

I walked inside and went directly to the guest room where my laptop and clothes were. I grabbed my stuff as quickly as I could. Glancing at the time, 1:02 pm, I closed my laptop and shoved it in the bag along with the charger. I dumped a laundry basket of clean clothes into a suitcase. When I turned to grab my medication from the bathroom, he came in the room behind me.

I turned. His eyes narrowed and his jaw clinched. He began screaming. He told me I was "worthless," "selfish," "fat," and "probably a cheater." I felt the situation escalating and decided to grab what I had already packed, find Ozzy, and get the hell out as soon as I saw a chance. But my abuser stood in the way.

"If I'm all of those things," I yelled, "why do you care if I'm leaving?"

My question sent him over the edge. He picked up the office chair in front of him and threw it on top of the desk. The noise echoed off every wall. Frightened, I stumbled backwards. Instantly, I knew I had to get out and quickly. I dropped my laptop bag and suitcase and ran toward the door.

The next thing I knew, I was lying on my back on the floor. He had thrown me to the ground with all his strength. Instinct told me I had to get up. I had to try to get away. As I tried to stand, he pushed me down to the floor again. My heart pounded; my muscles tensed as I fought for my freedom. He kept coming at me, shoving me down and laughing at my struggle. Every time I tried to stand, he knocked me to the ground. My wrists and hands hurt from landing on them over and over again.

Covered in sweat, I started to scream for help, hoping a neighbor would hear. Ignoring my cries, he pushed me so hard that my crashing body propelled the queen-sized bed across the floor and against the far wall. I was in danger. I had to find another way out. I set my sights on escaping out of the window behind me.

107

I clawed my way across the bed towards the window. If I could get it open, I could at least summon help. The window wouldn't budge.

I was trapped; fear engulfed me.

My abuser stood in the middle of the room and taunted me. Suddenly he came barreling towards me and I knew I had to act. I kicked through the window shattering the glass with my right foot. I crawled over the shards, screaming. I made it halfway out when he grabbed my legs and yanked me back into the house. He flipped me over on the bed and put his hand over both my mouth and nose. He kept repeating, "Shut the fuck up" over and over. He straddled me with his heavy body; his knees dug into my hips. I flailed and thrashed, trying to escape, but he was too big. I struggled to breathe. Every time I could catch my breath, I screamed and hoped someone on the street would hear me.

His eyes locked on a pillow lying beside my head. Immediately, I froze and stopped yelling. If he put the pillow over my face, I knew I would die. He removed his hands from my mouth and nose and put them on my shoulders. I was completely pinned down.

"Please, let me go," I sobbed. I begged over and over but he was unmoved.

"You broke a fucking window, you stupid bitch," he screamed in my face as he foamed at the corners of his mouth.

He looked like a different person; someone I had never seen before. His eyes were dark and the veins in his face and neck bulged.

He's going to kill me.

"Please let me go," I begged again.

"Shut the fuck up, you stupid bitch," he screamed.

This is it. This is what my gut has been warning me about. He's a monster and will do anything to keep me under his control. If he can't control me – he's going to kill me.

I made a choice. I could lie there and hope he would tire or get bored and let me go. Or, I could try to escape.

I chose to fight for my life.

I took a sharp breath and felt the adrenaline flow through my shaking body.

"Get off of me right now, or I am going to fight back," I whispered.

"Do it," he hissed, inches from my face.

Although he was pinning me down on the bed with his body weight crushing my legs and his hands pushing my shoulders into the bed, I realized his face was close enough to me that I might be able to scratch him to get him to release me. I tensed my left hand and dragged my nails down the left side of his face. Shocked, he grabbed his face with both hands, freeing me to move my upper body. I punched at him and landed a blow just under his eye. The jab knocked him off balance. I freed my left leg and drove my left foot into his mouth. I cried out with every blow. Even in such a perilous situation, I didn't want to hurt him. Despite it all, I still loved him.

The kick knocked him onto the floor. I jumped up and shouted for Ozzy as I ran through the house towards the back door with my laptop bag and small suitcase. I snatched my purse from the kitchen peninsula and pushed Ozzy with my inner thigh toward the back door.

I reached toward the handle.

I was so close to my escape. I just needed to get out the back door.

Suddenly, I was airborne and landed with a thud on my back on the hard linoleum kitchen floor. Startled, Ozzy ran into the dining room where I could hear him whining. My laptop bag, purse, and suitcase scattered on the floor beside me. My abuser crawled on top of me and covered my mouth and nose with his hands. I tried to scream, to move, to escape in some way but I was pinned.

"Look what you did to my face!" my abuser screamed. He spat blood onto my face and sweater. My favorite sweater, the one I had worn in our engagement photos. I screamed for help.

"Shut the fuck up! You're going to fucking jail for kicking me," he roared as he moved his hands from my face to my neck and squeezed.

"Look what you're doing to me," I whispered as I gasped for air, clawing at his hands to release me. "You're going to kill me!"

"Shut up!" he screamed again, his hands still around my neck. He banged my head against the hard floor.

My head ached from a lack of air and I could barely think. Dark orbs started to contort my vision. He was so much bigger, and I was losing energy. He was just too big for me to overpower.

"Ozzy!" I managed to gag out. "Ozzy, please."

I heard the click of nails along the hardwood and then on the linoleum. I strained, trying to turn my head to the side. Ozzy was next to me

109

facing my abuser. He snarled and exposed his teeth. He was ready to attack, and my abuser knew it.

Reacting in fear, my abuser jumped off me, cursing at both Ozzy and me as he retreated into the darkness of the house. I scrambled to my feet, threw my laptop bag over my shoulder along with my purse, and grabbed my suitcase and Ozzy. Together we ran out the backdoor, down the stairs, and toward my SUV.

I'm going to get away.

I put Ozzy in the back of the vehicle, ran to the driver's side, and started the car. Suddenly my abuser jumped into the passenger side of my car.

"Get out," I yelled.

He grabbed for the keys and tried to pull them from the ignition. I punched and slapped at his hands. He recoiled.

"Get the fuck out of my car!" I screamed as loudly as possible.

"Look at my face!" His nose was almost touching mine. Blood spewed from his busted lip and gums onto my face. "You're going to jail, you fucking bitch."

I grabbed for my purse and somehow got hold of my cell phone. I jumped out of the car and pretended to call 9-1-1.

"Hello," I shouted to no one on the other end, "my fiancé has attacked me and he's trying to kill me." I ran to the back of the vehicle and he followed. He chased me and grabbed for my phone.

"Hang up." His voice was a roar.

"Yes, his name is..." I started to say and spelled his name into nothingness.

"Bitch!" he screamed. But he finally stopped following me.

In that brief second of hesitation, I jumped back into the car, threw it into reverse, and careened out of the driveway. I had made it. I had escaped. I looked at the clock, it was 1:22 pm.

The longest and most dangerous afternoon of my life had lasted only twenty minutes.

Getting Out

For Kendall Ann, leaving her abuser was one of the hardest but most important moments of her life. It is difficult to comprehend how someone who claimed to love her could inflict such venomous rage and violence towards her. Reading her story can be incredibly challenging for many reasons. The last moments with her abuser were terrifying. There was no guarantee she was even going to get out alive. There were many instances prior to her escape where she could have left, potentially avoiding the violence and trauma she endured. However, once someone is being actively abused, their emotional state can alter, making it more difficult to leave.

"Why not get out?"

It can be difficult to understand why Kendall Ann's relationship went on long enough to become as dangerous and violent as it did. Perhaps her experience resonates with the one you are enduring or have already left. That is why the issue of leaving safely must be addressed. Most survivors of abuse make more than one attempt to leave. Often their abuser uses a tactic called *hoovering* to reengage the survivor in the relationship. This is accomplished through tactics of repair, such as in the honeymoon phase of abuse. Kendall Ann's abuser made one last hoovering attempt when he made her favorite meal to extend a manipulative olive branch. Other forms of manipulation found with hoovering include using bargaining chips such as; children, family opinions, religion or reputation. *Hoovering* is a **Red Flag** indicative of an abuse cycle that needs to stop.

Getting out is not easy; sometimes it is not safe, and there will almost always be difficulty with the process. Often the longest stage of leaving an abusive relationship is the pre-contemplative stage. This is the first stage of breaking an abuse cycle where the survivor has not yet had thoughts related to action but is in a place of "before thinking" about ending abuse of any kind. If you are still struggling with whether you want to leave, here are signs to consider about the state of your relationship, and whether you need to act and get out.

111

Signs That Your Abuser is *Not* Going to Change:

- They minimize the abuse or deny how serious it is
- They continue to blame others, or you, for their behavior
- They claim you're the one who is abusive
- They pressure you to go to counseling alone to fix the relationship instead of as a couple or by themselves
- They tell you that you owe them another chance
- They say they can't change unless you stay with them and support them
- They threaten to hurt themselves or you if you leave
- They try to get sympathy from you, your children, or your family and friends

Addiction to an Abuser Who Won't Change

It is important to remember that an abusive relationship can present with some of the same characteristics as addiction. There are highs and lows in most addiction cycles, and recovery does not begin until responsibility is taken, or admission of powerlessness to the addiction is expressed. In the case of intimate partner violence and other forms of abuse, it would be ideal for the abuser to take responsibility for their actions. As we explored previously, blame is often misdirected onto the survivor of abuse as opposed to the abuser. The reason? If the abuser takes responsibility, they fear the risk of losing the control they possess that keeps their abused partner connected, reliant and essentially addicted to the relationship. Ironically, taking responsibility and ownership for wrongdoings represents the safe and effective way to keep a partner and resolve conflict.

Many abusers lack insight about their issues and rarely are given a proper diagnosis or treatment to help address their disordered personality types or substance abuse patterns. Many of them never end up attending therapy where they could be provided much needed insight into their behavior patterns and relationships. The likelihood of full recovery from a personality disorder, such as narcissism, sociopathy or anti-social personality disorder, is rather low. People with such disorders tend to lack insight or self-reflection.

112

While the abuser may be less likely to seek out help, survivors often possess more awareness of their need for help and support. Despite their willingness to receive such support, the controlling nature of the abuse makes it difficult for survivors to feel safe about seeking out the help needed to aid in leaving their relationship. Often the most important decision for survivors of abuse who want to change their lives, is whether or not to leave. This is a decision that cannot be arrived at with the help of the abuser, which is why fighting against isolation and seeking out support from those outside of the relationship, such as when Kendall Ann reached out to her cousin, is crucial.

When you do feel ready to explore leaving, we want you to be equipped with how to do this as safely as possible. The following section will explore how to navigate some of the issues that can arise when trying to leave an abuser. We will also explore how Kendall Ann handled her own escape. You will learn actions you can take to increase the odds that you will get out safely, with the hopes of preventing the same type of trauma Kendall Ann endured.

Asking for Help

When Kendall Ann met her cousin for lunch, she shared her plan to leave. Her cousin's concern about Kendall Ann's safety was both extremely valid and foreshadowing. Kendall Ann's desire to leave was immediate and driven by fear and resolve. It was certainly time for her to get out, but doing it alone increased the risk of her enduring further abuse. The result was the violent, traumatic, and frightening scene you just read.

This does not have to happen to you. Although there are no guarantees when it comes to leaving an abuser, there are a number of things you can do to increase the likelihood of getting out safely. Even if you are not currently ready to leave, it is best to learn what you can do (such as a safety plan), because if the situation escalates, it may be too late to create a strategy. Kendall Ann experienced the consequences of not having a safety plan. The time between her telling her cousin she was leaving and the moment she left for good was less than 24 hours. Even more remarkable, it took only minutes for violence to erupt once she entered the house. From there she had to fight to survive. There is a much safer way to leave

113

"Asking For Help"

This exercise is intended to explore your history with seeking help. Identifying your ideas and narratives about asking for help makes it easier and more likely that you will reach out when you need it most.

1. When I was younger, who did I reach out to when I needed help and how did they react?

2. If I do, in fact, struggle with asking for help, at what age do I recall starting to have a hard time doing so, and what was going on in my life?

3. What do I think about people who ask for help from me or others?

Brene Brown, an influential researcher on topics of shame, courage, and vulnerability, explored courage in her *Netflix* special, *The Call to Courage* (2019). In it she referenced a quotation from a speech Teddy Roosevelt gave in 1910: "You can't really be brave without vulnerability." What your abuser has put you through has already demanded a great deal of courage. Enduring abuse is no small feat. Now it is time to be brave enough to be vulnerable; it is time to ask for help.

Seeking Support

Involving a support person may be necessary for leaving safely, and we *strongly* encourage you to ask for help from someone you trust. If you have struggled with asking for support in the past, consider this quotation by the motivational speaker, Les Brown: "Ask for help. Not because you are weak. But because you want to remain strong."

Whenever possible, get involved with people and activities outside your home. Having a pre-established support network helps when the time to leave arrives. **A great deal of safety planning relies on the support of others**. If your abuser has maintained the power of control over your social life, building a social network can be difficult. In this case, even just one safe person, maybe a co-worker (which Kendall Ann reached out to and sent the strangulation photos to) who your abuser does not have contact with or a medical provider who can offer both expertise and support, can make a significant difference.

The Pre-Planning Stages of Leaving

Whether or not you are ready to leave, there are still steps you can take to protect yourself. These safety measures can make the difference between your getting out safely, or not getting out at all.

Safety Measures

Know your abuser's personal **Red Flags**. Stay alert for signs and clues that your abuser is getting upset and may explode in anger or violence. Come up with several believable reasons you can use to leave the house (both during the day and at night) if you sense trouble brewing.

- **Identify safe areas of the house:** Know where to go if your abuser attacks or an argument starts. Avoid small, enclosed spaces without exits (such as closets or bathrooms) or rooms with weapons (such as the kitchen). If possible, head for a room with a phone and an outside door or window.

116

- **Come up with a code word:** Establish a word, phrase, or signal you can use to let your children, friends, neighbors, or co-workers know that you're in danger and they should call the police.

Holding on For Too Long

The longer you stay in this *pre-planning stage*, the more likely your body will start to internalize a state of hypervigilance once you leave the relationship. As previously mentioned, *hypervigilance* is an enhanced state of sensory sensitivity accompanied by exaggerated efforts to detect danger in your environment. Hypervigilance can bring about a state of increased mental and physical anxiety and exhaustion, which can result in various medical issues brought on by chronic inflammation. It is not uncommon to experience an exaggerated startle response as a result of hypervigilance.

Examples of being in this state for too long include; an increased sensitivity to loud noises, anxiety around large groups of people (especially people who are unknown), and a sensitivity to stimulating environments, even if the noises or spaces are technically safe.

Because support is an integral part of leaving an abusive relationship, having a trauma response in the presence of people can be very limiting. Isolation creates a much smaller world as you avoid seemingly dangerous situations, and it can limit the number of people you can access for support. It also makes it more difficult to be independent and in control, thus making it easier for your abuser to maintain power.

This state of heightened stress is also one of the common traits associated with Post-traumatic Stress Disorder (PTSD), which can develop as a result of severe or prolonged abuse. It is important to understand that maintaining safety by being on guard can provide a false sense of stability and calm. This appears in Kendall Ann's story when she says she would comply with what her abuser wanted and be temporarily rewarded for her efforts. For example, when she folded laundry the way he demanded as opposed to having her own voice and way of living. A false feeling of safety can create a sense of tension and anxiety while waiting for the abuser to erupt again.

This false sense of safety and peace is part of the abuse cycle, explored in Chapter 2 in the Power of Control Wheel. This stage of the abuse cycle is called **Calm**, which is when you must remain hyper-sensitive to your partner's mood to keep the peace. This is all while they are restricting their true abusive tendencies before the next eruption. Many would describe the efforts to maintain this calm as a period of "walking on eggshells." Such brief moments of calm demand a lot of psychological energy to keep the tension low and the fighting at bay. You deserve to be in a relationship where you do not have to hold the flood gates closed and sustain peace through your own psychological efforts.

Your Exit Plan

Devising an exit plan can help when negotiating your way through a violent or abusive relationship. Kendall Ann shared how the physical abuse in her relationship began so abruptly that she felt confused and shocked. She was filled with questions and doubt as she tried to comprehend how her abuser could go from never being physically violent to straddling and strangling her. It felt jarring, and difficult to organize her exit strategy when she was dealing with emotions connected to the violence. Her exit plan only started to take shape when she spoke with her cousin. Her cousin warned her that going back to her home alone was dangerous, and her cousin was right.

Leaving on your own can put you in danger.

We hope this book can help protect you from the potential of any further abuse when you decide to follow through with leaving. As previously mentioned, an important step to promote safety is creating a plan. We *strongly* encourage you to create your own **Personalized Safety Plan**. Some of the following questions may be outside the scope of your situation, such as whether or not you have children, but we want to cover as many contingencies as possible. It can also be helpful to ask a trusted counselor, friend, or other professional to help you draft the plan. It might also be wise to involve them in the safety measures.

Not everyone is ready to include others in their safety plan, as outing an abuser can be complex. Regardless, there are still many strategies you can put into place immediately.

Personalized Safety Plan

STEP 1: Safety during a violent incident.

I can use some of the following strategies:

A. If I decide to leave, I will:

(Practice how to get out safely. What doors, windows, elevators, stairwells, or escapes would you use?)

B. I can keep my purse/wallet and car keys ready and put them (location)_____, so I can leave quickly.

C. I can tell _____ about the violence and request that she/he call the police if she/he hears suspicious noises coming from my house.

D. I can teach my children how to use the telephone to contact the police, the fire department, and 911.

E. I will use _____ as my code with my children or my friends, so they can call for help.

F. If I have to leave my home, I will go to _____.

G. I can also teach some of these strategies to some or all of my children.

H. When I expect we're going to have an argument, I'll try to move to a place that is low risk, such as _____,
_____, _____
_____, and _____.

119

(Try to avoid arguments in the bathroom, garage, kitchen, near weapons, or in rooms without access to an outside door.)

I will use my judgment and intuition. If the situation is very serious, I can give my partner what he/she wants to calm him/her down.

STEP 2: Safety when preparing to leave.

Victims frequently leave the residence they share with the battering partner. A careful exit plan increases safety. Batterers often strike back when they believe their partner is leaving a relationship.

I can use some or all of the following strategies:

A. I will leave money, an extra set of keys, and clothes with _____
_____.

B. I will keep copies of important documents or keys at _____
_____.

C. I will open a savings account by _____ to increase my independence.

D. Other things I can do to increase my independence include:
_____
_____

E. I can keep change for phone calls on me at all times. I understand that if I use my telephone, the following month's phone bill will show my batterer the numbers I called after I left. To keep my phone communications confidential, I must either use a pay phone or use a cheap burner phone kept in a secure place.

F. I will check with _____ and _____ to determine who might let me stay with them or lend me some money.

G. I will sit down and review my safety plan every _____
in order to plan the safest way to leave the residence.
_____ (domestic violence advocate or friend's name) has agreed to help me review this plan.

H. I will rehearse my escape plan and, as appropriate, practice it with my children.

120

STEP 3: Safety in my own residence.

There are many things someone can do to increase safety in their own residence. It may be impossible to do everything at once, but safety measures can be added step by step.

Safety measures I can use:

A. I can change the locks on my doors and windows as soon as possible.

B. I can replace wooden doors with steel/metal doors.

C. I can install security systems including additional locks, window bars, poles to wedge against doors, an electronic system, etc.

D. I can purchase safety ladders for escape from second floor windows.

E. I can install smoke detectors and fire extinguishers for each floor of my house/apartment.

F. I can install a motion-activated outside lighting system.

G. I will teach my children how to make a collect call to me and/or to _____ (name or friend, etc.) in case my partner kidnaps them.

H. I will tell the people who take care of my children which people have permission to pick up my children and that my partner is not permitted to do so. The people I will inform about pick-up permission include:
_____ (name of school)
_____ (name of babysitter)
_____ (name of teacher)
_____(name[s] of others)

I. I can inform _____ (neighbor) and_____ (friend) that my partner no longer resides with me and tell them to call the police if he/she is observed near my residence.

STEP 4: Safety with an Order of Protection.

Many batterers obey protection orders, but one can never be sure which violent partners will obey and which will not. I recognize I may need to ask the police and the courts to enforce my protective order.

The following are some steps I can take to help the enforcement of my protection order:

A. I will keep my protection order _____ (location). Always keep it on or near your person. If you change purses, that's the first thing to go into the new purse.

B. I will give my protection order to police departments in the community where I work, in those communities where I visit friends or family, and in the community where I live.

C. *There should be county and state registries of protection orders that all police departments can call to confirm.* I can check to make sure that my order is on the registry. The telephone numbers for the county and state registries of protection orders are: _____ (county) and _____ (state).

D. I will inform support persons such as my employer, friends, family, religious leaders and/or _____ , that I have a protection order in effect.

E. If my partner destroys my protection order, I will get another copy from the clerk's office.

F. If the police do not help, I can contact an advocate or an attorney and leave a complaint with the chief of the police or the sheriff.

G. If my partner violates the protection order, I can call the police and report the violation.

STEP 5: Safety on the job and in public.

Everyone must decide if and when they will tell others that their partner has battered them and that they may be at continued risk. Friends, family, and co-workers can help to protect you. Each person should carefully consider which people to invite to help secure their safety.

I might do any or all of the following:

A. I can inform my boss, the security supervisor, and _____ at work.

B. I can ask _____ to help me screen my telephone calls at work.

C. When leaving work, I can _____
_____.

D. If I have a problem while driving home, I can _____
_____.

E. If I use public transit, I can _____
_____.

F. I will go to different grocery stores and shopping malls to conduct my business and shop at hours different from those I kept when residing with my battering partner.

G. I can use a different bank and go at hours different from those kept when residing with my battering partner.

STEP 6: Safety and my emotional health.

The experience of being battered and verbally degraded by partners is usually exhausting and emotionally draining. The process of building a new life takes much courage and incredible energy.

To conserve my emotional energy and resources and to avoid hard emotional times, I can do some of the following:

A. If I feel down and am tempted to return to a potentially abusive situation, I can

_____

_____

_____.

B. When I have to communicate with my partner in person or by telephone, I can

_____

_____

_____.

C. I will try to use "I can ... " statements with myself and be assertive with others.

D. I can tell myself, "_____
_____" whenever I feel others are trying to control or abuse me.

E. I can read _____ to help me feel stronger.

F. I can call _____ and _____ for support.

G. I can attend workshops and support groups at the domestic violence program or_____ to gain support and strengthen relationships.

124

STEP 7: Items to take when leaving.

When leaving partners, it is important to take certain items.

Money: Even if I have never worked, I can take money from jointly held savings and checking accounts. If I do not, my abuser can legally take the money and close the accounts.

Here is a list of items to take with you. If there is time, the other items might be taken, or stored outside the home. It is advisable to put all these in a single location in case you have to leave in a hurry.

When I leave, I should take:

*Identification
*My birth certificate
*School and vaccination records
*Checkbook, ATM card
*Keys for house, car, office
*Medications
*Welfare identification, work permits, green cards
*Children's birth certificate
*Social Security cards
*Money
*Credit cards
*Driver's license and auto registration
*Copy of protection order
*Passport(s), divorce papers
*Medical records - for all family members
*Lease/rental agreement, house deed, mortgage payment book, bank books, Insurance papers
*Address book
*Pictures, jewelry
*Children's favorite toys and/or blankets
*Items of special sentimental value

Telephone numbers I need to know:

_____

Police/sheriff's department close to home

_____

Police/sheriff's department close to work

_____

Police/sheriff's department close to school

_____

Prosecutor's office

_____

Battered women's program (local)

National Domestic Violence Hotline: 800-799-SAFE
(7233) 800-787-3224 (TTY)

www.ndvh.org

Creating a safety plan can be very taxing, and it may bring up emotions and anxieties that you have potentially been trying to avoid. The plan itself is an enormous effort in self-care. Other forms of self-care are also essential for your safety plan. This is a time to be gentle with yourself and to find one thing, no matter how small, that you can do as an expression of kindness and self-love. Perhaps reviewing Chapter 4 (which outlines the Distress Tolerance skill of TIPP) would be helpful. It can also be beneficial to engage in other centering skills you enjoy such as meditation and exercise or activities that spark your creativity (writing, drawing, music, etc.). Sometimes in the midst of chaos and stress we forget these important skills. We will take an in-depth exploration into self-care in *Part II: Thriving*. For now, take a moment and breathe. Your breath is something that can anchor you at all times. You cannot breathe in the past; you cannot breathe in the future. Your breath only happens *right here, right now.*

What I Know Now

1. More than 70% of domestic violence murders occur during a departure or after the victim has gotten out.

This is a sobering statistic that I was completely unaware of when I left my abuser. I didn't know the danger I was in when I was attempting to leave. I assumed he would probably call me names and say horrible things, but I did not think he would attack me with such violence. I was completely vulnerable and without a plan. I was flooded with emotion and all I could think about was leaving, but I didn't consider the obstacles. I wish I would have known the importance of planning ahead and including my support system. I now know that having a well-planned exit strategy could have prevented the trauma that impacts me to this day. Leaving an abuser is dangerous. He could have seriously injured or killed me during my escape. When I walked into our home, I had no idea I was walking into a battle for my survival. The situation would have been worse if there were children involved, so having a safe exit plan would be even more important if there were children to be protected.

2. It is often crucial to get a restraining order or order of protection.

After I left my abuser, he stalked me for some time. He also tried to manipulate me into feeling guilty for leaving him. I was hesitant to pursue a protective order because I was nervous it would antagonize him into more violence. Each state differs in protective orders procedures, so it's important to understand what obstacles you'll need to overcome.

To get a protective order against my abuser, I had to go to the courthouse and fill out paperwork describing the abuse I had suffered, revealing why I was still fearful of my abuser. I had to meet with a judge in his chambers and discuss the same information. (Some states allow you to meet with the judge virtually) I then had to take the signed order to another floor to get another signature. Next, I took the order to the basement of the courthouse and delivered it to the state police who served it to my abuser. Yes, I had to confess my abuse to four different people after standing in four different lines. I had four chances to change my mind. Each of these steps was difficult and I second guessed myself at every turn. I was not aware there would be so many steps, so I did not take anyone with me, which was a mistake. It would have been reassuring to have someone's hand to hold during the process. After the initial order was granted, I was given a court date for a hearing on extending the order for a year. My abuser chose to fight the order, which meant I had to testify in court about what he had done. My father came with me to court that day and I am forever grateful for his support during the ordeal. It was embarrassing to have to tell another judge and a room full of strangers the hell my abuser had put me through, but in the end, it was worth it because the order was granted. In court on the day of my hearing, I watched several women who had been granted temporary restraining orders decline to pursue year-long orders. For me, that was not an option. I had to protect myself from my abuser.

The judge also ruled that Ozzy would be protected by the order because I was fearful my abuser might steal him and hurt him for revenge.

I hadn't known anyone who had gotten a restraining order before, so I didn't know how much the process entailed. Here is the bottom line: *it's not the easiest process to navigate, but it's not the hardest either!* You can do it. Someone once told me that the restraining order was "just a piece of paper" and I understand their perspective. For me, however, that piece of paper added a layer of protection I desperately needed. It also gave me a reason to broach the subject with individuals who could help protect me. I gave a copy of the order to the leasing office at my apartment and to the HR Department at my job. Instantly the circle of people keeping an eye out for my safety grew and I didn't feel as alone.

Please visit https://www.thehotline.org/ for more information on restraining orders.

3. I should have involved the people I trusted in my leaving.

When I made the choice to leave, I still hadn't told anyone but my cousin about the abuse I was experiencing because I didn't truly understand the terrible level of danger I was in. I planned to tell my friends and family what I had been through once it was over. I didn't expect my abuser to attack me when I left him, so I didn't think it was necessary to include my support system until I was out of the relationship. *This was a mistake*. I wish I had told more people that I was going to leave my abuser, and the reasons. Maybe someone would have known how dangerous my decision was and warned me to take the steps outlined in this chapter to protect myself. Isolation was a powerful weapon in my abuser's toolbox, and it affected the way I chose to leave him. If I had told someone about the abuse I was suffering before I left, I believe the situation would have been dramatically different and, more importantly, safer.

What Do You Know Now?

*This section is intended for you to convey your thoughts,
feelings and reflections on what you learned in the chapter by writing
or using other creative forms of expression.*

Chapter 8

The Aftermath

"*Trauma creates change you do not choose; healing creates change you do.*"

In the moments right after driving away from my abuser, I came to the first stop sign and finally took a deep breath.

Then, I screamed.

The noise of my own howl was unrecognizable, the depth of its pain immeasurable. The sound choked in my throat from the weight of my tears. I slammed my hands on the steering wheel, then lay my head on it, sobbing. *This isn't real. That didn't happen.*

Surely, I would awaken from this nightmare at any minute. A honk from the car behind me jolted me back to reality and I inched my car through the intersection. I didn't know where I was going, or where I would be safe. My mind raced.

He almost killed me. Ozzy saved me. Is he following me? How did that happen? Holy shit. He almost killed me. He almost killed me.

"He almost fucking killed me!" I screamed, tears soaked my sweater and shirt.

I broke a window. Oh my god, I kicked out a window. I broke a window in a house I don't own. He's going to tell everyone it's my fault. He's going to lie. No one is going to believe that he's a monster. He's going to say I kicked out a window for no reason. Shit. I need to tell his stepmother what I did. It's her house. I need to tell her, so he doesn't lie.

131

I grabbed my phone and dialed his stepmother's number. I needed to admit I was the one who broke the window and promise to pay for it. I needed her to know the truth.

"Hello," she answered sweetly.

"I kicked out a window in the guest room of your house," I screamed into the phone.

"What?"

"He was strangling me and choking me, and I kicked the window out to live," I shouted.

There was a pause.

"Oh, Honey," she finally replied, "We thought you cured him of this."

It was a punch to the gut.

"What?"

"Honey, he has a history of this. His ex told my daughter that he hit her in the face, and we know he locked her in a bathroom on a family vacation," she confessed. "But we thought he was being better for you."

"Why didn't you tell me this before?" I wailed into the phone.

"I thought he grew out of it," she answered.

"I need to go," I responded as rage enveloped my body. "I will pay for the window." I hung up the phone.

Again, I screamed.

His family knew. They knew he was violent. They knew he was dangerous, and they didn't warn me. The betrayal was too much to stand.

I pulled my car into a gas station parking lot and called my sister. I spewed out what had happened.

"Has he ever done anything like this before?" she asked.

I was quiet. Would now be the moment that I shared the awful truth?

"Yes," I responded.

"Come home," she whispered.

My hometown was hundreds of miles away, a twelve-hour drive. But home was also where my mom, dad, sister, and brother were, the people I trusted most.

"Okay," I responded. I put the car into drive, and I began the journey.

132

Twelve hours later, Ozzy and I walked into my mom's house and I fell into her arms. Her face was anguished. I could tell her heart was breaking for me. I told her some of what happened, but my soul was too tired, and I needed to sleep. During the night I heard her creep into the room and stare at me. She was making sure I was still breathing the same way first-time parents check on their sleeping newborn babies. The next day I told the truth. The horrible, dirty secrets I had been keeping poured from my throat. The name calling, the forced sex, the strangling. Everything. My mom didn't flinch. She held my hand and whispered that I wasn't alone anymore, and we'd make it through this nightmare together.

Telling my brother, sister, and father the truth was equally as painful but was met with the same loving understanding my mom had displayed. The mantra was the same: "You're not alone anymore. We'll get through this as a team." I felt lucky to be able to tell them what happened without fear of judgment.

I did not answer my abuser's texts or calls for several days. I was too upset to confront him in any capacity. While out to lunch with my father, my phone buzzed repeatedly. My abuser had sent me hundreds of texts and was now calling dozens of times in a row.

"Is it him?" my dad asked quietly.

I nodded.

"Want me to answer it?" he said reaching out his hand.

I smiled but shook my head. Even as a grown woman it felt reassuring to have my dad offer to protect me.

I knew I would have to answer my abuser's calls and texts at some point. I needed him to understand the wedding was off and the relationship was over. The thought of speaking to him frightened me, even though he was hundreds of miles away. Later that night, my mom agreed to sit next to me and hold my hand while I called him.

I dialed his number and put him on speaker. I found the strength to recite the words I had practiced with my mother. "The wedding is off, and we are no longer in a relationship," I told him.

I could feel his rage through the phone. "I gave you a ring and you made me a promise," he bellowed. "We are getting married."

My mom's eyes widened as she heard the anger in his voice. I could tell it made her scared for me. She shook her head at me.

133

"No, we are not," I said and hung up.

For several days I stayed at my mom's house trying to make sense of what had happened.

One morning I stood naked in front of the full-length mirror in my mom's guest room and inspected the bruises on my body. I ran my hands over them, flinching in pain. The origins of many of the marks were easy to identify. The handprint on my arm where he grabbed me. The scrapes and bruises on my legs from the broken window where I tried to escape. Each mark told the story of what I had survived. I wondered if the bruises on my hips were from when he had been on top of my body in the bedroom trying to suffocate me or when he was strangling me in the kitchen and beating my head on the dingy linoleum floor.

The trauma of what I had experienced settled on my soul and I stumbled backward distancing myself from my image in the mirror. I couldn't catch my breath. I slid down the wall behind me, sobbing. How much longer would I have to endure this excruciating pain? How many more days? How many more hours? Minutes? Seconds? I lay in a heap on the floor for what seemed like an eternity. I could not find the strength to pull myself from the tile. If given the choice, I'd have stayed there forever. I didn't know how I would face the challenges ahead of me, but I knew if I lay there long enough my mom would soon come to check on me with a gentle knock and soft voice. I couldn't allow her to see me this way.

I dragged myself from the floor and sat on the bed. There were things I needed to do. I had a wedding to cancel. I had a job to keep. I had a loyal dog to care for. I had family and friends waiting for me, wondering how they could help. But I wasn't ready to tackle any of these seemingly insurmountable challenges. I thought about crawling into the bed, pulling the blankets over my head, and melting into a warm, deep cocoon. Again, paralyzing agony consumed me, and I sobbed with such violence that no sound escaped my body.

Worried about my distress, Ozzy barked and brought me back to the present. I walked back to the mirror and stared at the bruises on my hips again. They were deep purple and blue surrounded by green and yellow halos. In that moment, I made a promise to myself. I'd only let what he had done hurt me while my body displayed his viciousness.

When the bruises faded, I'd live again. I just had to be strong until the evidence disappeared from my body.

I was committed not to let what I had been through destroy my life, so I left the safety of my mom's house and returned to the apartment I leased the day I left my abuser. I had to continue my job. My plan was to find new employment in my hometown as quickly as possible and move back closer to my family.

In the following weeks, the bruises on my body were my "happiness timeline." Once those bruises vanished, I'd be better. Each night, I scrutinized their progression. The self-reporting of my discolored body preserved my sanity. I marveled as they changed from blue and purple, to green, and then to yellow. One day, they finally disappeared.

But my emotional pain did not retreat.

The first time I went to the grocery store after leaving my abuser, the task of making even the smallest choice sent me into a panic. I stood paralyzed in the soda aisle looking at the cans and bottles. The world around me started to spin. *I need to sit down.* I heard my heartbeat in my ears, and I struggled to breathe. *I'm going to pass out right here in the middle of the store.* I sank to the floor and sat in the middle of the aisle, struggling to catch my breath.

"Miss," a young man knelt beside me. "Are you okay?"

"I don't know," I cried.

"Should I call 9-1-1?" he asked.

"No, no, no," I replied.

He scanned my face.

"Are you buying soda?" I asked through tears and shortened breaths.

"What?" he replied.

"Are you buying soda?" I repeated.

"Yeah," he said, looking confused.

"Are you buying cans or a two-liter?"

"Two-liter," he answered. He was still noticeably confused; I was crying and struggling to breathe while asking him about soda choices.

By now several employees had surrounded us and my breath had slowed. They helped me to my feet and implored me to let them call an ambulance. I refused and gathered what little dignity I could muster. I walked to my car where I sat for what seemed an eternity and wept. I couldn't even decide what soda to buy anymore. I needed a stranger to help me. That's when it occurred to me how the years of fearing my abuser's displeasure had left me incapable of making even the smallest decision on my own.

Weeks after my bruises disappeared, my soul still yearned to be freed from the torment of heartache, disappointment, and betrayal, but still no noticeable change occurred. I was haunted and I was angry. I was not the type of woman to fall apart. I was strong. I was tough. Why couldn't I conquer this? Why couldn't I just move on?

I thought maybe getting out of my new, sparsely furnished apartment would ease my mind, so I made plans to visit my best friend. Days before the visit I started to feel tired and nauseated. I visited Urgent Care and the doctor who examined me expressed concern.

"You have strep throat," he said as he sat in the chair across from me. "Your throat is raw, and you have a very high fever. Why did you wait so long to come in?"

"I didn't even know I was sick," I replied sheepishly.

"How in the world could you not know you were this sick?"

The question hung in the air. I knew why. Every day was a battle; simply existing was difficult enough. I was disconnected from my body because the weight of what I was carrying was simply too much. The doctor prescribed a strong antibiotic, and I spent the next several days in bed trying to repair my body and my heart.

One morning, the sound of my phone ringing in the next room startled me from a daze. I hustled to it and answered. During that conversation, a sound emerged from my gut, something I hadn't heard in weeks. A laugh. Although a brief moment of respite from my misery, its effects were permanent. It showed me that "happy" still existed in my body. Maybe there wasn't a time restriction on healing after all. Maybe as long as I knew there were still things to laugh about in the world, there was hope of recovery. Maybe recovery was about surviving the day and searching for the moments of peace within it. Whatever the case, I was ready to find out.

Defining Trauma

Simply being alive and being human makes us susceptible to trauma and it can have devastating and lasting effects on our mental and physical health. *Trauma* is defined as the response to deeply distressing or disturbing events that overwhelm an individual's ability to cope. What Kendall Ann experienced was nothing short of traumatic. Her life had been in danger and her agency over her own body had been threatened. Trauma can cause feelings of helplessness, diminishing one's sense of self while reducing the ability to feel a complete range of emotions and experiences. Essentially it can make us feel numb.

To heal from trauma, it is essential to treat yourself with patience and compassion. The amount of time it takes to heal is different for everyone. Rushing the process can aggravate the symptoms of trauma and prolong the ability to feel healthy and whole again. When Kendall Ann declared that she would feel better, no matter what, once her bruises healed, she was not giving herself the time and space needed to process her trauma. We encourage you however, to take all the time you need to process any trauma you have endured. One important aspect of processing trauma is gaining a greater understanding of what happens when someone endures trauma, helping to normalize your experience. For that reason, the rest of this chapter provides important information regarding different forms of trauma and symptoms of PTSD.

Developmental Trauma

Trauma is often not one single incident. Instead it can be a series of events or dynamics in a relationship that break down your sense of safety and self-worth over time. This is also known as "complex trauma," which originates from abuse in relationships of any kind, whether it be parental abuse, intimate partner violence, or abuse in other interpersonal relationships.

Complex trauma is the exposure to varied and multiple traumatic events, often of an invasive, interpersonal nature. Kendall Ann's relationship was an example of complex trauma that can result in Complex Post Traumatic Stress Disorder (CPTSD). There was not one specific trauma as a result of the different forms of emotional abuse and power of control her abuser put her through. For this reason labeling one event in the relationship as a "trauma" can be difficult when the relationship as a whole is the trauma.

Disrepair of trusting, healthy relationships is a key trait of complex trauma. Trauma is not always done at the hand of a violent person nor is it always a threat to physical safety. Some forms of trauma stem from a lack of love, understanding, or encouragement from those who matter to you most. I once worked with a client who was reflecting on a past traumatic relationship that she struggled to label as "abusive" because it was mainly verbal and emotional abuse that she experienced. She expressed that because the abuse never became physical, it was difficult for her to recognize how serious it was until it was too late. Once abuse occurs, the likelihood of developing a trauma response increases and there are various ways in which people respond.

Pete Walker, a licensed psychotherapist and author, described four different trauma responses that survivors of complex trauma experience in his book; *Complex PTSD: From Surviving to Thriving*. These trauma responses can be elicited by a number of triggers and can impact how the survivor experiences future relationships. It is normal to display more than one type of trauma response at any given time and for them to surface in different types of scenarios or relationships. Here is a brief overview of each response as outlined by Walker.

Fight: "These types learn to respond to their feelings of abandonment with anger and subsequently use contempt, a toxic amalgam of narcissistic rage and disgust, to intimidate and shame others into mirroring them and into acting as extensions of themselves."

Flight: "Flight types appear as if their starter button is stuck in the 'on' position. They are obsessively and compulsively driven by the unconscious belief that perfection will make them safe and loveable. When the obsessive/compulsive flight type is not doing, she is worrying and planning about doing."

Freeze: "The freeze response, also known as the camouflage response, often triggers the individual into hiding, isolating, and eschewing human contact as much as possible. This type can be so frozen in retreat mode that it seems as if their starter button is stuck in the 'off' position. It is usually the most profoundly abandoned child – 'the lost child' – who is forced to 'choose' and habituate to the freeze response."

Fawn: "Fawn types seek safety by merging with the wishes, needs and demands of others. They act as if they unconsciously believe that the price of admission to any relationship is the forfeiture of all their needs, rights, preferences and boundaries." This type is often seen in codependent individuals, which often attract narcissists, and for that reason will continue to be a focus throughout this book.

Single Incident Trauma

Acute trauma results from a single incident. For example, being a victim of or witnessing a violent crime or natural disaster or being involved in a car accident that does not result in ongoing, life altering changes for the individual. (It is important to note that if the traumatic event results in pervasive negative effects, such as paralysis, the trauma would likely be categorized as "chronic trauma")

Acute trauma is associated with events that are markedly different from everyday life. Unfortunately, when someone experiences a more chronic form of trauma, such as in a long term abusive relationship, some of the trauma inducing events becoming normalized, internalized, and chronic.

Symptoms of PTSD

When we encounter an event that elicits fear, our body is prehistorically designed to react quickly. It does not take minutes to respond. Instead the brain starts pumping out cortisol within three seconds of a trauma trigger. High levels of cortisol in the body over a long period of time can reduce muscle mass and bone density, increase wrinkling in the skin, and cause degradation of digestion. The impact of trauma on an otherwise healthy brain brings up the question of how we understand trauma and its treatments.

Trauma should not be labeled as mental illness, rather it is a form of mental injury that can result in other mental illnesses if it goes untreated. Too often trauma is overlooked as the primary issue and misdiagnosed for other mental illnesses. Trauma clients often enter therapy with a laundry list of disorders; depression, bi-polar, multiple person-alities, substance abuse, and eating disorders to name a few. When all of those diagnosis are stripped away, at the core you will often find trauma. One diagnosis made from a collection of symptoms constitutes a syndrome. PTSD can be viewed in much the same way. With PTSD there is a common syndrome of criteria present in most sufferers.

- **Exposure to a traumatic event** (Your abusive relationship qualifies as such)
- **Re-Experiencing Symptoms** (Reliving the event)
- **Hyperarousal Symptoms** (Restlessness, feeling high-strung, jumpy, keyed up, hypervigilant, or uneasy)
- **Avoidance Symptoms** (Avoiding situations, locations, and/or people that remind you of the traumatic event)
- **Negative changes in your beliefs or feelings** (You may start to have a negative sense of self as well as negative beliefs about others in your life, which can extend to a negative worldview)

Just as there is no specific way for someone to experience trauma, there is no specific way in which PTSD symptoms present. There are, however, criteria and symptoms that are present in most people with PTSD. You do not have to be a war veteran or a victim of natural disaster to develop PTSD. Trauma also does not have to happen directly to you; there are instances of secondary trauma after witnessing another person's endangerment. Burnout in law enforcement is an example of secondary trauma that often goes untreated. PTSD is not a disorder that develops without the cause, i.e. the traumatic experience. But some people are more likely to present with symptoms based on their unique past and resiliency, which will be explored further in *Chapter 9 Avoiding Future Abuse.*

Trauma and the Brain

After the immediate danger of a trauma event passes, our brain can still react as if the event is imminent. *Thinking* about a traumatic event, such as abuse in its many forms, can elicit the same physiological responses as the actual event. Reactions can include a change in breathing rate, sweating, dilation of pupils and constriction of muscles.

Human beings are innately driven towards attaining safety and security. This drive for safety can be altered in the brain of someone who has endured trauma. Historically, the school of psychology deemed the brain as being hardwired circuitry that had a prime time for maximum learning, followed by a regression in the ability to change and learn thereafter, respective to age.

Further research has found that the brain is much more malleable in its ability to learn and grow. *Neuroplasticity*, a term first used by Polish neuroscientist Jerzy Konorski in 1948, focuses on how neural pathways and synapses in the brain change due to behavior and environment. The saying, "use it or lose it," describes what happens during something called "synaptic pruning," which is the deleting of neural connections that are no longer necessary or useful, and strengthening the necessary ones. Without synaptic pruning, our brains would not be able to prioritize what is most important to us, such as learning the language spoken by our family and those in our community. What we repeat, our brain believes is important, even if it happens to be an unhealthy thought pattern or behavior, much like playing the same groove on a record. The more it plays, the deeper it becomes.

Repetition of certain post trauma responses can "trim away" the parts of the brain that are responsible for achieving relaxation, play, and interpersonal effectiveness in exchange for neural connections responsible for survival and self-preservation. If someone endures an abusive relationship, the neural pathways related to stress, fear, self-protection, hypervigilance, and mistrust will be reinforced while the pathways bolstering close relationships, healthy risk-taking, and trusting others grow weaker.

The good news is that even though the brain can curtail these connections, they can be rebuilt.

Reaching Out

An excellent form of self-care for surviving trauma is finding community, support, and contact with others. For some this may mean joining a group dedicated to addressing trauma for survivors of abuse; for others it could be getting involved in hobbies or interests such as a community choir, a self-defense class, or joining a local yoga studio. Attaining these connections and social bonds can make a difference in the way your brain heals from trauma. Often it is not until someone feels a sense of community that they can truly start the healing process.

To help establish your support group for thriving after abuse, we would like to invite you to join our reader group. This online group is a space where you can hear from other readers who may be able to relate to your personal story. You can find the link to our reader group at the author's websites at, www.ameliakelley.com and www.kendallanncombs.com. In addition to the reader group, your own family, friends, therapist or other helping professionals can also become part of your community. When the time feels right for your journey to begin, we are here.

"Genetics are like a score of music, and environment is like the conductor. Just because you have a certain set of keys present in your score of music does not mean all those notes (or genetic markers) will be played or turned on."

~ Bessel Van de Kollk ~

What I Know Now

1. Abusive relationships are a form of chronic trauma for survivors.

It wasn't until I began discussing what happened in my relationship with my therapist that I came (with her help) to the realization I had been abused. She asked me, "Do you self-identify as a survivor of domestic violence and abuse?" My first reaction was, "No!" After several more conversations with her I started to understand I had in fact experienced serious trauma from my relationship. I was so focused on putting it behind me and not letting my abuser have any more control or influence in my life that I wasn't giving credence to the trauma I had experienced. When I recognized I had lived with someone who was trying to control me through verbal abuse, sexual abuse, and violence, I could then begin to work on the aftermath.

2. Your body might know you have PTSD before you do.

Early in my recovery I went to a carnival with my mother, niece, and nephew. It was very crowded with many people in all directions and lots of unpredictable noises. Immediately, I felt dizzy. Although I was hundreds of miles away from my abuser and he would have no reason to know my location, I was suddenly frightened that he would appear and I would not be able to protect myself or, worse, be powerless to protect my family.

Nearby, at a game booth people were shooting water into the faces of plastic clowns. They were trying to blow up balloons attached to the clowns' heads. As we walked by the game, a balloon popped with a loud bang. The noise sent me into a tailspin. I began sweating profusely and I thought I was going to have a heart attack. I had no idea this was a symptom of PTSD and I was fearful I'd spend the rest of my life afraid to be in public and scared of loud noises. Through therapy I learned many different grounding techniques to help me in these situations. Even now, loud unanticipated noises can elicit a trauma response from my body, but I have learned how to settle myself.

143

3. I thought I was going to be negative forever.

Before I met my abuser, I was a happy person. Although I tended to be more anxious than the average person, I was genuinely cheerful on most days. For a time after I left my abuser, I struggled to see the world as a positive place. I felt I should be fearful of everyone's intentions and suspicious of anyone who tried to be nice to me except for family and close friends. Worst of all, I felt like I could never be happy again because if I let my guard down and enjoyed happiness to any degree, the world would see it and something bad would happen. It was a lonely, sad time. I transformed from a woman who would be the first to celebrate any of my achievements into someone who worried that anything positive could be easily stolen by unpredictable circumstances. The belief paralyzed me.

Luckily, life proved me wrong. Yes, sometimes great things turned out not so great, but many times they turn out better than expected and I relearned that the world can be just as beautiful as it is scary. Now I revel in every small victory because I know the world isn't waiting to take away my happiness the minute I let my guard down. Life is so much better when I allow myself to be happy without fear.

What Do You Know Now?

*This section is intended for you to convey your thoughts,
feelings and reflections on what you learned in the chapter by writing
or using other creative forms of expression.*

Part 2: Thriving

Chapter 9

Avoiding Future Abuse

"Self-reflection is the school of wisdom."
~ Baltasar Gracian ~

**Due to the complex nature of trauma and abuse, this chapter will
focus on therapeutic insights without a narrative from
Kendall Ann.***

Safety is imperative for survival. Understanding how to avoid
dangerous situations and people is essential for maintaining our well-
being. Once someone has experienced abuse or assault, their chance of
re-experiencing a similar type of trauma increases. Although this may
seem grim, it is not the entire story. There is hope, as there are ways
to reduce the chances of abuse reoccurring and we want to empower
you with this knowledge. Awareness and proactive self-care can help
to increase your resiliency and help you maintain healthy relationships.

As we have discussed in the previous chapter, trauma changes
the brain. Unfortunately, these brain changes can result in a survivor
being more likely to endure abuse in future relationships. For many
survivors, this is counterintuitive. Most survivors never wish to experience the agony of abuse again and resolve to avoid any further abusive
situations. Despite a strong desire to remain safe, changes in the brain
after abuse can make it more difficult for the nervous system to regulate
stress. When our stress response never shuts down, we remain in the

149

fight-flight response, which can make it difficult to feel comfortable in stable relationships because the brain becomes adapted to stress.

This can be shocking information for survivors to process and some feel hopeless after learning it. However, employing certain strategies and techniques will help reduce how these changes impact future relationships.

Processing Self-Blame

It is common for survivors of abuse to blame themselves for the unacceptable behaviors of their abuser. Abusers will gaslight and blame their partners for their own abusive behavior. Often an abuser will say, "You made me do this" in an attempt to transfer blame from the abuser to their victim. One reason why this form of manipulation and emotional abuse is so effective is because it helps alleviate stress for the victim if they feel like they can do something to affect change in the relationship. Taking blame can also reduce the victim's pain when trying to reconcile how someone they trusted or loved could do something so horrible to them.

As mentioned, assuming responsibility for the abuse can make a survivor feel that they have the power to end the abuse cycle. By taking blame for the abuse (for instance thinking, *If only I did not make them so angry,* or, *next time I will listen and stay out of their way*) the abused deflects blame away from the abuser. When victims take blame for the abuse, it often leads to the relationship lasting longer than it should. Self-blame is a dangerous thinking pattern that increases the likelihood of future abuse occurring in that or other relationships. A healthier thinking pattern would be focusing on what it means to be safe.

There is a primal need for safety and normalcy involved with these unhealthy trauma bonds formed during an abusive relationship. As human beings we have a perception that what is familiar is **safe** and what is unknown is **dangerous**. This belief becomes problematic when what is familiar is actually the dangerous relationship and what is unknown and feels more frightening is leaving the abusive relationship. For this reason it is essential to clearly define safety and to focus your attention on attaining that.

Defining Safety

Being exposed to an abusive relationship creates somatic (physical) and emotional memories of what it felt like to survive the cycle of abuse. Memories related to regaining safety from an abuser provide a memory of relief that can make it difficult to remember the periods of danger and instability. Because of this cycle, it is more likely that once someone is abused, the likelihood of ending up in a relationship with a future potential abuser increases.

Establishing expectations about safety is crucial when forming healthy relationships. To create a foundation for safety, you can reference these top six traits for safety that we recommend for every healthy relationship:

- **Trust and honesty** – the absence of gaslighting
- **A healthy social network** – support from those outside of the relationship is encouraged
- **Individuality and self-confidence are encouraged**
- **Open communication and striving to understand one another**
- **Anger management and fighting fair** – no one ever feels fear when in a conflict
- **Healthy sexual relationship** – consent is always the central focus

Resiliency

Resiliency is defined as the capacity to recovery quickly from tough situations. Building your resiliency is essential when trying to break the cycle of abuse. Applying the thriving skills that will be explored in the next section is an effective way to support yourself and increase thriving after an abusive relationship.

Part of resilience training is learning to decrease negative thoughts and instead bring greater focus to the things that matter most to you. Enduring an abusive relationship over a period of time can cause an impaired stress response. This can reduce resilience factors that help us us make healthy relationship choices. It is essential to refocus on emotional, cognitive, physical and spiritual resilience when moving on from an abusive relationship and towards healthier and safer ones in the future. The following five pillars of effective resilience can help to prevent future abusive relationships from occurring.

Pillar 1 Self-Awareness

Self-Awareness means having a clear perception of your personality, including strengths, weaknesses, thoughts, beliefs, motivation, and emotions. Self-Awareness allows you to understand other people, how they perceive you, your attitude and your responses to them in the moment.

Pillar 2 Mindfulness

Mindfulness is a state of active, open attention on the present. When you're mindful, you observe your thoughts and feelings from a distance without judging them as good or bad. Instead of letting your life pass you by, mindfulness means living in the moment and awakening to experience.

Pillar 3 Self-Care

Self-care is unique for each person and can be understood in many different ways. In its simplest form, the term refers to our ability as human beings to function effectively in the world while meeting the multiple challenges of daily life with a sense of energy, vitality, and confidence. Self-care is initiated and maintained by us as individuals – it requires our active engagement.

Pillar 4 Positive Relationships

Positive Relationships include the people who support and care for us – and we care for them. One of the most profound experiences we can have in our lives is the connection we develop with other human beings. By building positive relationships with others, we will be happier and more fulfilled because we feel more supported and connected. Positive, supportive relationships improve our overall immune health and lead to more satisfaction with our lives.

Pillar 5 Purpose

Purpose is a recognition that we belong to and serve something bigger than ourselves. Our purpose helps to shape the mindset and attitude we have toward others and the events we experience. Some examples of where we can find purpose is in our work, faith, family, a political party, or being a part of an organization that matters to us.

By strengthening these pillars, you become more resilient. Instead of experiencing a trauma response when encountering stress, these five pillars work together to lift you out of the chaos. In this section on *Thriving*, we will be paying special attention to resilience and offer tools that are efficient, easy and simple to use. These skills are designed not only to help you thrive after an abusive relationship, but also to reduce the likelihood of future abusive relationships.

Pillar 6 Shame Resiliency

Shame associated with staying in an abusive relationship can increase the likelihood that someone will not leave the relationship. It is important to reiterate that abusive relationships *are not your fault.* One of the most important aspects of shame resilience is *honesty.* Brene Brown speaks about how sharing your shame story with a safe person can actually reduce the power of shame. Clients I have seen in my clinical practice have provided evidence for this. They are less likely to maintain unhealthy relationships when they do not keep the details of their relationship secret but rather reach out for support. Sharing our shame is important as it reduces the emotional load. With reduced emotional stress, the likelihood that you will continue making unhealthy choices lessens.

If you do not feel ready to share these feelings with someone who knows you or your abuser well, it can also be helpful to reach out to a therapist or some other helping professional. There are several resources where you can anonymously locate a therapist in your area. One is *Psychology Today*, which can be found at www.psychologytoday.com. If you are experiencing a more urgent crisis, the FCC recently designated a three-digit number to reach the National Suicide Prevention Hotline: 988.

There is great value in finding someone who is safe, objective, and knowledgeable to help you through this part of your journey. An important factor in finding value in therapy is whether you connect with your therapist and have a good relationship. If you have had negative experiences with therapy in the past or found it to be unhelpful, perhaps you could take a chance on a new therapist. Allow yourself to be very selective and take your time finding the right fit.

Whether the answer for healing is to look to the past for insight, or to the future for direction, one thing is true, it comes down to control. A survivor of abuse who has been controlled by their intimate partner can be left feeling powerless, and that is where the repetition of abuse occurs. Taking back your power and deciding to leave unsafe situations is essential in reducing the chance of experiencing a future abusive relationship. Leaving an abusive relationship, much like Kendall Ann did when she drove away for the last time, creates a new narrative of power in your future choices.

What I Know Now

1. I believed that if I tried harder to please my abuser, I could stop the abuse.

Throughout my life, making people feel loved and supported was my currency in relationships. I can recall in high school always trying to be the person who ran to the rescue of any friend having drama or heartache. I carried this behavior into my adult romantic relationships. I believed that if I loved my abuser harder or better, he would stop being mean to me and the "old him" would return. The cycle of abuse cemented this unhealthy pattern of behavior for me because when I doted on him, he responded positively. His behavior, however, was unpredictable and would change quickly. In my mind I was the one who was causing his behavior and so I also had the power to change it. I would spend all of my mental energy figuring out how to be perfect for him so he would love me and not be cruel. I took the blame for his unacceptable behavior because he would tell me it was my fault and I believed him because I thought I needed to be perfect to be loved in a healthy, stable way.

2. Shame is isolating.

I have close family and loyal friends who have been by my side for decades but guess how many people I discussed my abuser's behavior with before I left: zero. I told no one because I was ashamed of what was happening to me and I was fearful that people would love me less if they knew what my abuser was doing to me. I believed they might force me to leave him before I was ready. I also worried that if he got better and I stayed, they would begin to hate him. I worried they may blame me for what he was doing since he told me it was my fault most of the time. What if they thought I was stupid for staying? I took on the burden of his actions for years in order to keep his secret. I didn't realize that allowing the shame to dictate my decisions was isolating me from them, which in turn made my abuser and me even more connected. He was the only one who knew what was happening.

Although now the people who love me most (and those reading

155

this book!) know a lot of what happened to me in my abusive relationship, there are things I still do not share with them, and that's okay. You are not required to tell everyone every detail of the misery you survived. There are certain details that only my abuser and I know. Even my therapist, who knows a great deal, does not know everything that I endured. You get to decide what you tell and to whom. You must do what is best for you.

3. I had a head start on my "resiliency journey".

If the definition of resiliency is the capacity for overcoming tough situations, then there is no one more resilient than abuse survivors! Most of us were constantly forced into painful situations to keep the peace. The five pillars of resiliency, self-awareness, mindfulness, self-care, positive relationships, and purpose, are all important in giving you back something that you may have lost during your abusive relationship: your voice. Strengthening these five pillars make it easier to speak your mind and create the happy, hopeful life that you deserve. Figure out who you are and what you believe (not what your abuser told you to believe). Observe your thoughts and take note of any patterns and decide if those patterns still serve you. Take time to care for your beautiful soul. Cut out people in your life who are toxic, or don't respect your boundaries. Put your energy into something that stirs your passion. These are the actions that have kept me moving forward to create the life that I want!

What Do You Know Now?

This section is intended for you to convey your thoughts, feelings and reflections on what you learned in the chapter by writing or using other creative forms of expression.

Chapter 10

The Nothing

*"Even a happy life cannot be without a measure of darkness,
and the word happy would lose its meaning if it were not
balanced by sadness. It is far better to take things as they
come along with patience and equanimity."*
~ Carl Jung ~

For the first several weeks after I left my abuser I was on an adrenaline high. Although I was still stuck in the city where my abuser lived, I was determined not to let his actions destroy my life and I made a commitment to move forward without exception. I spent each day clinging to the thought that he would not break my spirit. If I had survived his abuse without surrendering, then I could rebuild my life now. It was "white knuckle" survival. I was holding on as tightly as possible to the conviction that my life wouldn't be ruined by a manipulative, abusive man. My righteous anger buoyed me in those first weeks. I ignored the pain and lived up to my responsibilities. Those who knew what occurred in my relationship routinely stated that they were in awe of the strength and resiliency I was demonstrating.

As much as I tried to maintain my forward progress, one emotion kept creeping into everything I did: fear. I was living while holding my breath. Each time my phone rang or beeped I was fearful it was my abuser or one of his enablers. The incoming email notification on my laptop made me nauseated. Even with a restraining order to protect Ozzy and me, the terror was pervasive.

I limited the number of times I took Ozzy outside and changed our routine daily so it would be impossible for my abuser to predict. Each time I walked outside I was armed with pepper spray in case my abuser was lurking. Although I lived in a gated apartment complex with great security, I was frightened to leave my apartment and fearful my abuser would break in and steal Ozzy as he had once threatened. I made mad dashes to a nearby gas station to buy Frosted Flakes and milk and had a week's worth of pizza, soda, and sandwiches delivered from the nearest pizza shop.

"I'm so fucking scared," I whispered into my cell phone to my best friend, Gretchen.

My fear made me angry. I was angry with my abuser. I was angry with the people who enabled his behavior. And I was angry with myself for staying with him and possibly endangering Ozzy and me.

But there was another emotion I was trying to escape: the love I still felt for my abuser. Why was I missing the man I had fallen in love with years before? How could I miss a man who had sexually abused me? A man who had strangled me. A man who had called me "fat," "a bitch," and "disgusting." A man who had lied constantly, who had tried to turn me against the people in my life who cared deeply for me. A man who had suffocated me and slammed my head on a kitchen floor. What was so wrong with me that I would still long for a man who did such terrible things?

I hated my abuser, and I was starting to hate myself.

It was too much, so I shut my feelings off. I made a choice to ignore my emotions. It was easier to be numb than to deal with the fear, anger, and love that overwhelmed me.

My choice invited something new into my life, numbness and depression. I called it *The Nothing*. I got the name from a 1980's movie, *The Never Ending Story*, where a strange phenomenon called "The Nothing" destroys all color and hope from the land, leaving devastation and sadness.

The Nothing engulfed my life. Somehow it made life simultaneously impossible and easier. I was no longer afraid of every noise, but I was unmotivated to do even the most basic tasks. The only comfort I found was lying on my bed and crying into Ozzy's fur as I used him for my pillow. Although he was my greatest source of comfort, I couldn't find peace. Had my abuser hurt Ozzy when I wasn't around to protect him? I held Ozzy closer and wept at the thought that I hadn't protected him.

Some days I found the strength to eat whatever was in my apartment; other days I couldn't even find the motivation to drink water. Many days I didn't brush my teeth or change my clothes. Every couple of days I made my way to the shower where I sat on the tile and sobbed while hot water ran over my body.

I had heard of people dying from a broken heart, and I started to believe it was possible and that it was my destiny. I worried I'd never live a normal life again. The damage, the heartbreak, the depression would make it impossible to be happy.

I thought about making the pain go away permanently. I could take a bottle of pills, never wake up, and finally escape this soul crushing agony. Then I thought about my mom and all the people that loved me. Plus, I couldn't leave Ozzy when he had protected me; it was my turn to protect him. I'd be escaping my own pain but transferring it to others and I couldn't bear the thought of hurting the people I loved.

I was ashamed of my depression, so I told no one. When talking on the phone with my friends and family I lied and painted the picture of a woman who was overcoming abuse and moving on with her life. In reality I was entrenched in my pain and unable to see a way out. My abuser was going to win. Although I cared enough for my well-being (and Ozzy's) not to go back to my abuser, he was still controlling my life.

Each day I struggled to complete even the smallest of tasks while knowing there were monumental undertakings ahead. It was hard to imagine finding a job in my hometown much less moving across the country when I could barely keep up with my basic self-care. These were things too challenging to face for a person who couldn't even find the strength to shower.

I did the bare minimum for my job each day. I knew I'd be quitting and moving home, so I wasn't concerned about being reprimanded or fired. Since I worked from home I was able to work for only a couple of hours each day without anyone noticing. I simply didn't have the strength to be productive.

Despite *The Nothing*, Ozzy had saved my life and I refused to neglect him. While previously we walked at least three miles each day, the distance seemed impossible now. Our new routine was to go on three separate one-mile walks every day. While in our apartment, Ozzy never left my side. Many times while I was showering he'd push the curtain back with his snout so he could see me. It was as if he knew how fragile I was becoming.

The Nothing made me exhausted but unable to sleep. I'd lie awake all night reliving every traumatic event in my relationship, sobbing into Ozzy's fur, asking God to relieve me from this pain. I'd go days without sleeping, which added to the brain fog induced by *The Nothing.*

One afternoon after three nights of no sleep, I put Ozzy in my car (because I was terrified of going anywhere without him) and drove to the nearest pharmacy. I bought several bottles of over-the-counter sleep aid and an allergy medicine that I knew made me tired. That night I took the sleep aid and managed to get four hours of shut-eye. When I woke, I lay in bed hoping I'd gently fall back to sleep. Instead, I was met with the memories of what my abuser did to me and spent the rest of the night crying and clutching Ozzy for comfort.

The next night I decided to take one and a half doses of the sleep aid. The result was six hours of sleep. I maintained this sleep schedule for about one week, but soon I needed more medicine to replicate the results. I started to take both the sleep aid and the allergy medicine to achieve six hours of sleep.

Sleep was my only escape from *The Nothing*. It was the only time I didn't see my abuser's face: eyes red, nostrils flaring as he choked and suffocated me. This lead me to want to sleep all the time, even if *The Nothing* was making it difficult. I needed to escape, so on weekends I started taking the sleeping pills during the day.

In the morning when I woke up I'd take Ozzy for a mile walk and then take my sleep concoction. I'd usually wake up around 2 PM, take Ozzy for his second mile walk, and take another dose. That would cause me to sleep until 8 PM when I'd take Ozzy for his third and final mile. Then more pills to sleep through the night. I repeated this every Saturday and Sunday for several weeks.

One Monday morning I woke up and walked into my closet to get my sneakers to walk Ozzy when I noticed something hanging in the corner: a white garment bag. I took it into the bathroom, hung it on the shower rod, and unzipped it to reveal my wedding dress. As I ran my hands down the organza it occurred to me that I'd never get the chance to wear this beautiful garment, the dress my mother had so generously purchased for me out of love. My mind raced as I thought of the day we'd bought it and my mom's delight when she saw me in it for the first time. Now the dress was nothing but the physical embodiment of a dream that would never be.

I fell to the floor and cried. I had to get this thing out of my apartment.

I walked to my desk and opened my laptop. I typed "Sell never used wedding dress" into Google and found a site where dress owners posted their dresses for others to buy at discounted rates. The only problem was I needed to take pictures of myself in the dress.

I grabbed my phone. "Christine," I said to my cousin, "I need your help."

We made plans for her to take photos of me in the dress to post. There was only one problem. I couldn't stomach the thought of putting on the dress. Christine and I decided there was only one way to solve the problem: alcohol. The following Sunday we went to brunch where I drank my weight in bottomless mimosas and then headed to my apartment to take the photos.

While wearing the dress I felt like I was being suffocated. No amount of champagne could numb the pain. I wasn't headed to my wedding. I was trying to get rid of the damn dress. As always, Christine's positive and comforting manner got me through the event.

Within a week the dress had been sold. I took it to my local UPS store to ship it.

As I lifted the dress onto the counter I started to cry.

"It's okay, my friend," the kind man behind the counter said. *"You're going to be all right."*

You're going to be all right. It was a simple sentence, but it provided me with immense hope. I might not be all right now, but I was going to be.

That night as Ozzy and I sat on the sofa and watched tv, I glanced

163

over at a pile of boxes. Inside were all of the wedding gifts from my friends and family. "Fuck," I said out loud. *What am I going to do with gifts for a wedding that will never happen?*

The man at UPS's voice echoed in my head. *You're going to be all right.*

I walked over to the pile and picked up the first box. It was a beautiful bowl from a dear former work colleague. Keeping the gifts felt wrong. I grabbed some paper and a pen and wrote my friend a note thanking her for her kindness but explaining I couldn't keep the bowl. That night I found the strength to write three more notes to others who had so generously bought gifts and repacked the gifts into their boxes.

The next day I drove those four boxes to the same UPS store.

"You're back!" the man from the day before greeted me. "Feeling better?"

"No," I replied.

There was silence.

"I was engaged but my fiancé was abusing me, so I had to call it off." The words flew out of my mouth before I could stop them. "I have to return all of the gifts people bought us and it's horrible." I started crying.

"I will help you," the man answered.

I told him the names and addresses of each of the recipients, paid, and turned to leave.

"I'll be back with more tomorrow," I said over my shoulder as I pushed the door open.

"I will be here," he replied.

That night before I took my sleep aid regimen I wrote more notes. This time, I found the strength to finish five. I counted the rest of the boxes. If I continued to do five a day, I would be done in three more nights. So, that's what I did. Every note was difficult to write. I felt like I was admitting failure to those that loved me and I was ashamed.

Each night I'd write the notes and repackage the gifts. Each new day, I went to the UPS store where my new friend helped me ship them to their destination.

"This is the end," I said on the day of the final shipment. "What's next?" he inquired.

I paused. "I don't know," I answered.

"You're going to be all right," he said again with a smile.

That night I took only one dose of the sleep aid and was delighted to sleep six full hours. The act of sending those gifts back had stirred something inside of me. Although *The Nothing* was still dominating my life, I could feel it was beginning to lift.

The next day I wrote down three things I thought I'd be able to complete that day. They were easy tasks, apply to four jobs in my hometown (because four is my lucky number), do my current job for at least five hours, and "eat a damn salad."

To my surprise I was able to accomplish everything on the list. *You're going to be all right.*

The next day Gretchen called me to tell me that the company where she had recently been hired was looking for a sales rep...in my home state! In true best friend fashion, she had already called the Vice President of Sales and told him not hiring me would be one of the biggest mistakes he could make. Within a week I had a phone interview with him, and we scheduled an in-person interview for three weeks later. I continued to apply to other jobs (just in case) and soon I started to feel something new, hope.

My birthday was approaching. My cousin called to tell me that she was taking me out to dinner to celebrate. I pushed past *The Nothing* and told her yes. When I arrived, she had brought five of her friends to celebrate, too. I was having a birthday party. It gave me hope to see there were people in the world who cared enough to show up to a person's party they had never met just to lift her spirits. The love my cousin demonstrated in planning and executing such an event touched my soul. I wasn't alone. I was loved. *You're going to be all right.*

The Nothing was lifting. I was starting to smile again, starting to feel hopeful. Most nights I still needed to take medicine to sleep and clutched Ozzy for comfort, but I was no longer purposefully sleeping through my days to escape my pain.

But was I ready to face it?

I knew I had to talk to someone who could help me manage the trauma of what happened. I'd been in therapy for my anxiety since I was 18, so I understood the value in it, but still I was embarrassed to go back. My abuser had told me on many occasions that I went to therapy because I was "crazy" and "emotionally unstable." His comments made me stop

165

going during our relationship. I hadn't wanted to give him another weapon to wield against me. But he was gone now, and I knew I needed help. I had to get rid of *The Nothing.*

I called my family doctor and explained I needed a recommendation for a therapist. I was given five names. I didn't know if I had the strength to call all five. Luckily, the first on the list answered and I made an emergency appointment for the next day.

"Can I bring my dog?" I asked sheepishly. "I'm afraid to leave him at home because I've been through something bad."

"Of course," the secretary said sweetly.

The next morning, Ozzy and I got in my car to drive to my appointment, but I couldn't bring myself to start the engine. I didn't want to go. I wasn't afraid of her judging me or telling me something I didn't want to hear. I was afraid of revisiting the memories I was trying so desperately to avoid.

How do you explain to someone you don't know that you were disrespected, sexually abused, screamed at, choked, and suffocated? Where do you even begin? How do you express that you still miss and love the person that did those horrible things to you even though you hate him? What words can you possibly use to describe the terror you feel when you are anywhere without your dog because he's your safe space and your protector? How do you explain that your abuser's whole family knew he was dangerous, but didn't warn you? How do you find the words to describe how *The Nothing* is destroying you?

You're going to be all right.

I decided to drive to the building and sit in the parking lot. When I arrived I looked at Ozzy in the backseat.

"What do you think?" I asked him aloud.

As I looked at his sweet face, I thought of everything I had to live for. I unbuckled my seatbelt, got Ozzy out of the car, and walked inside.

It was time to kill *The Nothing.*

Cultivating Space for Your Healing Journey

Healing from abuse can be a long journey. There is no one specific path. Sometimes what will happen in the coming days, months, and years may not even feel logical. That is because you are trying to reorganize not only your life, but also your heart and your mind. You may experience feelings of growth and progress, quickly followed by feelings of regret, fear, and shame. One of the most important things to be as you move forward is curious. If you remain curious, you can quiet your critical mind and encourage growth. This process can often be uncomfortable and messy. You may find you need to invent a completely new path as you progress, and that takes time. To create your new path, it is important to maintain a safe distance from your abuser. Kendall Ann had a restraining order to ensure this, but not all survivors attain such boundaries.

No Contact Rule

An important way to create distance is by establishing a **No Contact Rule.** At this point, or in the near future, you may pursue legal action to obtain a restraining order or another form of protection. The no contact rule is in addition to any legal steps you may take. No contact is important because we are very responsive to our environment and those in it. Any exposure whatsoever to your abuser can make you vulnerable to their manipulation and abuse. We do not intend to create a sense of helplessness or to take away any of the power and strength you possessed when leaving. Instead we want to encourage you to keep your strength intact by maintaining distance and removing their influence over you all together.

No contact involves truly cutting your abuser out of your life. The following are important steps to establishing no contact, as well as measures to take if your abuser attempts to disregard boundaries you put in place.

- **No phone contact:** Block your abuser's number and/or change your phone number if necessary
- **No email:** Open a new email to which your abuser has no access and discontinuing use of your old email

- **No social media contact:** Block your abuser and/or shut down old accounts
- **Cut off relationships you shared:** No contact may also apply to those who are involved closely in your abuser's life such as their close friends and family members
- **Change your environment by altering where you go in the community to avoid running into your abuser**

Some of the no contact rules may already be covered in a restraining order, but these additional measures serve as good reminders for your own serenity and safety. Kendall Ann had practiced a number of these "No Contact" rules when she was in the beginning stages of thriving after leaving her abuser. She mentioned that she would change the location and regularity of where she and Ozzy took walks so her abuser could not predict where she was. She mentioned being careful about phone calls and emails and did not have contact with her abuser through social media, even though it was difficult at times.

Some of my clients have expressed resentment in having to change valued aspects of their lives, such as cutting off meaningful relationships. Letting go of a dear friend can be incredibly hard to reconcile; these changes often do not feel fair. Despite how difficult these changes can be, I remind my clients that some of the relationships they had during their abusive relationship may not turn out to be as healthy or supportive as they once thought. They often come to realize that they deserve much better once they get some distance from the life they had with their abuser. Finding your new independent life can be challenging, but it can also be a meaningful and therapeutic journey.

During the aftermath of leaving an abusive relationship, and while trying to maintain no contact, it is not uncommon for **cognitive dissonance** to return. It takes a lot to leave in the first place. Doubt and uncertainty will ebb and flow during this time.

Kendall Ann shared many moments where she missed her abuser and then was angry at herself for her feelings. It is important to remember that all of your feelings are valid. Being critical of your process will only harm you and lead you farther from the peace you deserve. Other factors such as children and family can dramatically increase the difficulty of these first stages of thriving after abuse. That is why it is incredibly important to sustain as little contact as possible, or better yet, none at all. This important separation ensures that your inner thoughts and feelings as well as the decisions you make about your life are yours and yours alone.

Dissociation From Pain and Depression

After leaving her abuser, Kendall Ann experienced many of the stages of grief commonly associated with loss. She mentioned feeling an adrenaline high and intense anger about how she had been treated by her abuser, she also experienced some extreme lows, sadness and the feelings of being numb. Her resolve to endure and to overcome her pain was strong and led her to what she called, "white-knuckle" survival. She used dangerous coping skills, such as medicating her pain so she could sleep and to shut out unwanted feelings. Medicating pain, without medical advice, is a sign that you may need additional support to help deal with your suffering.

When trying to thrive after abuse, feeling a sense of strength and power can be crucial for moving forward and letting go. However it is also important to have self-compassion, patience, and permission to show up for any feelings that arise. Kendall Ann mentioned how after a certain point, her intense emotions became too much, and so she chose to tune out from the emotions she was feeling. It felt safer and more manageable to be in *The Nothing* as she called it, as opposed to enduring the pain she was constantly experiencing.

When focusing on thriving we encourage you to show up for yourself just as you would support a loved one or a friend. Showing up for your emotions allows you to fully experience, process, and release any unwanted feelings that are preventing you from thriving. Unprocessed emotions can lead to depression, becoming "anger turned inwards." One of the symptoms of depression, *anhedonia* – the loss of interest in things you used to like to do – can feel a bit like *The Nothing*. It is difficult for your brain to discern between negative or positive experiences if you become habituated to being numb. If you regularly dissociate from negative feelings, being present when you want to experience positive feelings is much harder. This can create a sense of isolation even in the presence of others, which is a common thinking pattern of depression.

169

In contrast, over processed emotions can also be harmful and lead to both physical and mental health issues. It is difficult to find the right balance, especially without support from others, and that is why dissociating from the emotions altogether becomes a common method for coping. Dissociation generally develops when feelings become too threatening or overwhelming and can lead to parts of your mind and body feeling separated or turned off. Symptoms of dissociation vary but some common signs are:

- **Amnesia:** You might lose your memories of things that have happened
- **Depersonalization:** Feeling disconnected from your own body
- **Derealization:** Feeling disconnected from the world around you
- **Identity confusion:** You lose a sense of who you are
- **Identity alteration:** This means your identity may have changed. You might remember your old identity or not have any recollection at all
- **Loss of feelings**
- **Losing control of your body movements**

One of the most effective ways to help reintegrate is by bringing your awareness back to the present. Using grounding techniques that increase mindfulness can be very effective and bring immediate relief. Even though it can be difficult, showing up for your emotions increases your resilience and improves your distress tolerance. The more often you engage with your feelings in the present, the better you will become at dealing with stress in general. The next section will outline a number of grounding skills you can use to help reduce dissociation so you can remain safe and present with emotions as they arise.

Grounding Techniques

Kendall Ann mentioned a sense of uncertainty about being able to handle the pain once she chose to be present with it. Learning ways to tolerate being present with the pain can make these feelings more manageable. After trauma, it is normal to experience flashbacks, anxiety, and other uncomfortable symptoms. Grounding techniques help manage these symptoms by turning attention away from distressing emotions and refocusing your attention on the present moment. The following are research-supported grounding skills that can become part of your healing journey and can help you combat normal, everyday stress.

5-4-3-2-1 Technique

Using the 5-4-3-2-1 technique, you will purposefully take in the details of your surroundings and use each of your senses. Strive to notice small details that your mind would usually tune out, such as distant sounds, or the texture of an ordinary object. The following questions can be used to implement this skill.

What are 5 things I see?

Look for small details such as a pattern in the couch fabric, or the way light falls on the walls of the room you are in.

What are 4 things I feel?

Notice the sensation of clothing on your body, the sun on your skin, or the feeling of the chair you occupy. Pick up a nearby object and examine its weight, texture, and other physical qualities.

What are 3 things I can hear?

Pay special attention to the sounds your mind has tuned out, such as a ticking clock, distant traffic, or trees blowing in the wind.

What are 2 things I can smell?

Try to notice smells in the air around you, like an air freshener or freshly mowed grass. You may also look around for something that has a scent, such as a flower or an unlit candle.

What is 1 thing I can taste?

Carry gum, candy, or small snacks for this step. Pop a piece (or a bite) in your mouth and focus your attention closely on the flavors.

Categories

The next grounding skill includes a mental exercise that is discreet and easy to do anywhere. This can be done by choosing a category below and naming as many items as you can. Spend a few minutes to come up with as many items as possible. There are many more options available, but here are a few to try at the beginning.

- Movies
- Musicians
- Sports Teams
- Favorite Foods
- Animals
- Song Lyrics

Body Awareness

The next grounding skill is helpful when you may be feeling disconnected from your body due to flashbacks, panic, or physical tension. The Body Awareness Technique will bring you into the here and now by redirecting your focus to sensations in the body. Pay special attention to the physical sensations experienced in each step.

1. Take 5 long, deep breaths through your nose, and exhale through puckered lips.

2. Place both feet flat on the floor. Wiggle your toes. Curl and uncurl your toes several times. Spend a moment noticing the sensations in your feet.

3. Stomp your feet on the ground several times. Pay attention to the sensations in your feet and legs as you contact the ground.

4. Clench your hands into fists, then release the tension. Repeat this 10 times.

5. Press your palms together. Press them harder and hold this pose for 15 seconds. Pay attention to the feeling of tension in your hands and arms.

6. Rub your palms together briskly. Notice the feeling of warmth between them.

7. Reach your hands over your head like you're trying to reach the sky. Stretch like this for 5 seconds. Bring your arms down and let them relax at your sides.

8. Take 5 more deep breaths and notice the feeling of calm in your body.

Grounding Techniques © 2018 Therapist Aid LLC Provided by TherapistAid.com

Finding the Care you Deserve

As you continue in your thriving journey, we want to encourage you to find the care and support you deserve. Having a skilled therapist to share your experience with who only has your best interest in mind is an important part of thriving. This person should be there to hold space for you as you move towards a place of healing and peace. Most people begin receiving medical care from birth to ensure they are growing and developing in a healthy way. How might our society benefit if mental health became as normalized as other medical services?

In 2020, the COVID-19 pandemic highlighted the crucial importance of mental health. Before the world came to a halt, many people were functioning at full throttle and ignoring their own version of *The Nothing*. Overstimulated lives and "good enough" mental health were entirely too common. Many people would not attempt to reach out for help until a crisis occurred. Instead, we should be treating mental health as part of our journey, and by doing so we are honoring our own ability to thrive. We receive physicals and regular exams to rule out medical ailments. The same can and should be true for mental health.

Those who seek out counseling and make it a regular part of their routines end up living healthier and happier lives. Regardless, abusers will weaponize therapy as proof that their abused partners have "issues" and that there is something wrong with them. Kendall Ann's abuser used this form of gaslighting not only as a means by which to degrade her but also to maintain his power over her. Therapy can serve as a crucial tool for for self-discovery and change, which an abuser wants their partner to avoid because it reduces the abuser's power of control.

If you choose to take back your power and pursue therapy, there are practical things you can do to make finding a therapist easier. Prior to the onset of the pandemic in 2020, most insurance companies would not permit online counseling without special authorization. Fortunately, this has changed and telehealth, whether through video or phone, is highly accessible. There are companies whose business model is completely geared to accessible therapy from the comfort of your own home. This can be helpful when trying to overcome scheduling hurdles; it can also ease some of the anxiety with getting started. Kendall Ann mentioned feeling nervous leaving her house without her beloved protector Ozzy. This makes sense, and the right therapist will honor whatever you need to make you feel comfortable.

As mentioned in a previous chapter, www.psycholgytoday.com can be helpful when searching for a therapist. You can use qualifiers related to what you want to address in counseling such as; what type of insurance you have, and the cost of services. Therapists will offer a detailed profile with their photo to help you get a feel for them. Many offer free consultations or will be available to answer questions ahead of time through email or by phone so you can get a sense of whether they are a good fit for you.

If you would rather have support in finding the right therapist, you can check out a website such as www.betterhelp.com. This site prompts you to answer questions about yourself and create a profile after which they will provide you with a match. If at any time you wish to switch counselors, you can. Sites such as this are geared towards virtual forms of therapy and make getting help incredibly easy. Finding the support and care you deserve can offer ongoing gains towards thriving after your abusive relationship ends and for years to come. The many benefits that come from self-discovery and healing will lead to a greater sense of thriving during your journey after abuse. If you are feeling overwhelmed or suicidal, please call the National Suicide Prevention Lifeline at 1-800-273-8255.

What I Know Now

1. Feeling nothing isn't the same as feeling good.

When I was unable to sit with the upsetting and confusing emotions that I was feeling, I thought my only option was to turn off all emotions. This was a bad idea. Instead of getting me closer to healing, it delayed wellness significantly and introduced new problems. Managing the fear, anger, sadness, and confusion after an abusive relationship is a difficult task to undertake, but it must be done. Dissociating from those feelings is not a healthy or pragmatic method of dealing with those unpleasant emotions. While I was trying my best not to feel anything, I fell out of touch with everything going on around me. I'd have to check and recheck if I had completed tasks for work because I honestly could not remember if I had done them. The short-term memory loss was startling. I began writing a To-Do list and crossing things off when they were completed. At the end of the day on several occasions, I had to recheck the things on the list just to confirm they were completed because I had no recollection of doing them. Sometimes I would call friends and family without remembering I had already talked to them earlier. Now I know this memory impairment is a symptom of dissociation. After I resumed therapy and began processing my emotions, my ability to recall my days returned. As my emotions came back, so did my memory.

2. Grounding techniques work well!

Typically I use breath work to "bring me back to earth." If I find myself in a situation where I don't feel comfortable using my breath, the Categories Technique works well for me. My favorite category is "People I Love." I think of each person I love, and I call to mind something I love about them. I try to think of something new each time I use this strategy. Not only does this put me back into my body, but it also helps me feel grateful for all of the wonderful people I have in my life! Another grounding technique I use is to sing (to myself) one of the songs from my favorite movie, *The Wizard of Oz* (yes, that's why his name is Ozzy). Somehow thinking about the tune and lyrics helps to keep me grounded in my body when I am feeling emotionally flooded or when I can feel myself shutting down and disconnecting. I realize it is imperative for me to be present in my body.

3. Keep your eyes open for the good in people.

While fighting *The Nothing* I had several experiences where I was reminded that most people are good. I will never forget the man at the UPS store who showed me kindness during our interactions and his wise words of, *You're going to be all right.* He could see what I could not yet see; that I would get through my difficult time. His words buoyed me through one of the most difficult experiences of my life. I will also be forever grateful to my cousin for bringing her friends to celebrate my birthday because she knew I was struggling, and she wanted to uplift me. And I'll always remember her friends who treated me as one of their own even though they'd never met me previously. These experiences changed me. Because of those kind souls, I go out of my way to be kind to strangers – not just nice, but kind. I'm hopeful I can be a bright spot for someone who is struggling, even a stranger, so they can see the kindness that still exists in the world. When you're depressed it's easy to see the world as a hopeless place filled with cruelty, but if you can look for the light in people, you'll see that not everyone is as callous as your abuser.

What Do You Know Now?

This section is intended for you to convey your thoughts, feelings and reflections on what you learned in the chapter by writing or using other creative forms of expression.

Chapter 11

Your Journey Of Healing

*"You are allowed to be a masterpiece and a work in progress
simultaneously. "*
~ Sophia Bush ~

"If one more person tells me to take a bubble bath, I'm going to scream!" I said to my best friend over the phone. It was two months after I left my abuser, and I while I was no longer in the grasp of *The Nothing*, I was still not myself. I was dead set to find a new job in Maryland before quitting my current job and I felt stuck in every way. I was stranded in a city where I no longer wanted to live and far from all of my friends and family. I was scared my abuser would violate the restraining order meant to protect me. I was searching for a job that would allow me to move back to my hometown but was not making any progress, even after applying to what felt like hundreds of jobs.

"I have real problems. A bubble bath isn't going to do anything for me." I took a big gulp of my wine, desperate to erase the fear and pain living in my heart.

Wine had become my crutch. Every evening when I closed my work laptop for the day, I walked directly to the refrigerator and poured myself a glass of Pinot Grigio. Usually, I ended up drinking the whole bottle. I craved the third-glass lightness in my head and how it freed me from thinking about my abuser and what he had done to me. Despite the pain he put me through, I missed the good person I had fallen in love with, and I hated myself for it. When the alcohol kicked in, I felt

179

relief from the anxiety consuming my life, weightless and manic. I started to crave the mania.

I told myself that once I got over this rough patch in my life, I'd stop drinking. I just needed a few more weeks of the nighttime mania. I knew alcohol wasn't the best way to ease the crushing pain, but I needed the nightly escape. Each morning, I woke up feeling fine and was able to fulfill all of my daily duties. I was still excelling in my job, taking great care of Ozzy, and acting like a responsible adult, so I didn't see anything wrong with my bottle a night habit. It felt like the only thing I had to look forward to.

I had been a believer in therapy since I started addressing my anxiety when I was eighteen years old. Although I felt the need to make light of my reasons for going, "You get to talk about yourself for an hour and the person can't tell you to stop," I always loved the reflection and introspection of the process. When I sheepishly told my therapist about my wine drinking habit, she did not judge or admonish me. She simply asked if I thought I could maintain that lifestyle and whether drinking a bottle per night was getting me closer to my goals.

When I went home from the session, I didn't drink. It was challenging to resist the urge, and I realized I needed to find something else to ease the pain. While wine helped me escape, I came to realize the things that would help me heal would also force me to face my pain, head on. The thought terrified me.

Although I never considered myself particularly religious, throughout my life I had found solace in the act of going to church. On many occasions, sitting in a church and praying about what was causing me anxiety gave me a sense of control. It made me feel like I was doing something about the cause of my anxiety rather than just allowing the worry to haunt me.

The first time I went to church after leaving my abuser I knelt in one of the last pews. I looked up at the large crucifix above the altar. All I could do was cry. I felt abandoned by the God who was supposed to help me and watch over me. I began thinking about all of the unanswered prayers I had thrown upward during my relationship. Anger filled my body. I ran from the church and sat outside on the stairs as other parishioners entering the service walked past me.

"Guess church isn't going to be the new wine!" I said out loud as I started my car and drove away.

With wine and church eliminated from the *How is Kendall Ann Ever Going to Feel Better* list, I moved on to another old standby, exercise. I would set my alarm for 5:30 am and take Ozzy for a three-mile walk. After I dropped him off at my apartment, I would throw on my headphones and run another three miles. When I was tempted to grab some wine after work, I'd go to a dance class or to the gym and either lift or hop on the elliptical. By the time I showered and ate dinner I was so physically drained that I would fall into bed. Then, I'd repeat the routine the next day.

On the weekends, I'd hike, run, do hot yoga, go to the gym, or go to a fitness class. I was buzzing with anxious energy and I would do anything to keep from sitting still. When I was exercising, I'd be so preoccupied with the physicality of what I was doing that I didn't think of my abuser. After a while though, thoughts of him and what he had done would creep from the corners of my mind and soon my runs were spent obsessing over how to stop thinking about my trauma. There is a saying: *What gets ignored will come out sideways,* and this was proving to be true for me.

I told my therapist about my religious and exercise failures. She disagreed about "failing." She asked me what else I was doing for self-care.

"Don't tell me to take an effing bath," I snarked.

She paused. "How about yoga?" she asked. She wasn't listening.

"I told you I tried exercise, including hot yoga," I snapped.

She explained there were many different types of yoga and encouraged me to go to a class and concentrate solely on breathing. I told her that breathing was a huge component of the Bikram yoga class I was taking. It wasn't helping.

She smiled patiently. "I want you to go to another class, not a hot yoga class, and just concentrate on breathing."

If I am anything, I am compliant, so the next day I googled a "not hot yoga class" near me and soon I was sitting in a new studio. I moved through each posture concentrating on my breath. I finally felt connected to my body again.

As the teacher ended the class she gently said, "The light in me honors the light in you. Namaste."

I felt wet tears stinging my eyes. It was too much. I placed my head in my hands and wept. She walked over and sat next to me. "Yoga is a release for many people," she said placing her hand on my shoulder. "Whatever it is that is troubling you, let it out."

She sat next to me, hand on my shoulder for several minutes. Then she instructed me to lie on my back in the "Savasanah" pose; she lay by my side.

"Just breathe," she whispered.

I don't know how long we lay there but it felt like the first time I had taken a real breath in a year. Tears rolled down my cheeks and onto my mat. Finally, stillness swept over me.

"I'm ready," I told her.

I walked out of the studio feeling like a different person, but more like myself at the same time. When I told my therapist about my yoga breakthrough she smiled.

"I think you're ready for meditation!" she said exuberantly.

"If I could think of nothing, I wouldn't be here!" I retorted.

She handed me a small book about meditation and explained that the goal of meditation is not to think about nothing. The goal of my meditation would be to reconnect to my breath and my body. I took the book home, and began my meditation journey the next day.

The book instructed to me to try to mediate for five minutes every day. Each day it gave me something different to concentrate on. I concentrated on where my breath was in my body, sensations in my body, sounds around me, the feeling of my clothes on my skin. The book said my goal was to acknowledge any other thoughts I had during those five minutes, and then to allow them to float away as I refocused on my center of attention.

The only challenge was, it also told me to close my eyes. I couldn't do it. Somehow the act of sitting with my eyes closed invited unwelcomed memories. I saw his face, heard his voice, and felt him near me. The memories flashed through my brain like images in the flipbooks I had as a child. I needed a more positive image to concentrate on, so I printed out a picture of Ozzy and taped it to the wall. When it was time to meditate, I sat in front of the picture and gazed at it until it became blurry. Soon, I was able to sit in front of the image and soften my gaze immediately knowing the happy picture was close in case an unpleasant memory floated into my brain.

Most days it got a little easier and I began to love those five minute intervals of quiet. Soon, I was doing yoga several times a week and meditating every day.

I could feel myself changing, getting back to who I was before the abuse, before I was violated, before someone had tried to destroy me. I started to find peace.

One morning I woke up feeling stronger than I had in months. I jumped from my bed and pulled on my favorite yoga pants and tank top. I drove directly to the grocery store and filled my cart with all of my favorite things, the things I stopped buying because my abuser didn't like them. I looked at the contents of the cart and smiled. I walked back down the soda aisle, the scene of my embarrassing post breakup panic attack. I grabbed three, two-liter Diet Cokes and placed them into my cart.

"I prefer to drink soda from a glass instead of a can, so I buy it this way," I said to a nearby stranger.

"Um. That's great?" the person replied with a confused look on his face.

I chuckled and walked to the cashier.

At my next therapy appointment my therapist asked me how long it had been since I last drank a bottle of wine alone. I couldn't remember, so I smiled. "How about the last time you had a panic attack?" I smiled more. "Ahh." She grinned. "I guess you don't need a bubble bath after all," she added with a wink.

Preparing to Thrive

"To thrive in life you need three bones: a wishbone, a back-bone, and a funny bone"
~ Reba McEntire ~

While ending an abusive or unhealthy relationship, the body, mind, and soul tend to focus only on what is necessary, *surviving*. But now, in this phase of *thriving*, we invite you to pause for a moment, much like Kendall Ann did, to focus on your breath. Your breath, which is with you always, can offer distance from the stress you have been carrying in your body.

I once had a client ask me in session, *"Why do we need to use so many coping skills to be healthy? I feel like mental health is so much work!"*

It can certainly feel that way when you are first trying to change the way you think about self-care. Up until now, you may simply have been trying to survive the emotional strain of your abusive relationship. Throughout the work you will do in this section on *Thriving* (and specifically the sections on self- care), we encourage you to see the importance of integrating coping skills into your everyday life.

Some of these skills will be familiar, so these chapters may serve as a reminder of what you have previously done to combat stress prior to your abusive relationship. Self-care, otherwise known as self-parenting, is crucial to combat stress and trauma. The more stressed we are, the less likely we will be to begin a new healthy habit or to engage instinctually in coping skills. Practicing coping skills regularly makes them easier to maintain in times of extreme stress. What we repeat becomes important, and what is important to us becomes a *habit*. Habits happen without decision, such as brushing your teeth or buckling your seatbelt in the car. For this reason they do not require extra energy and can help to reduce the decision fatigue that occurs when trying to make major changes in your lives.

Where Do I Start?

A good place to start is by checking in with yourself about what you have done in the past that worked to reduce stress and increase wellness.

- What did I enjoy doing as a child?

- What is something I used to enjoy doing as an adult before things got bad in my relationship?

- What is something I always wished I could do that I have never done before?

Motivation For Change

It is important to remember that *motivation is not necessary* to start a new skill or behavior. You do not have to be motivated to do something good for yourself. For example, when my alarm goes off in the morning, I am very motivated to continue sleeping. But rather than staying in bed, I rise and meet the day, not because I am motivated, but because I am *committed* to being a mother, a therapist and a wife. A lack

185

of motivation is inaccurately blamed for why someone struggles to make a change. The issue is not *a lack of motivation*, rather it is a *lack of commitment*. What leads to success differs greatly for everyone.

If committing to lasting change feels overwhelming, it is often a symptom of our life situation or other issues with which we struggle. Some issues may include a lack of resources (such as time or finances), a lack of personal energy from caring for others, or mental/physical health issues. Regardless of what stands in your way, we continue to encourage and impress upon you the importance of regular self-care and re-parenting. For some it may be easier to think of starting the habit of regular self-care in *micro-goals* while for others it resonates more to have goals that feel robust and exciting. Whichever works better for you, removing the barrier of self-doubt and focusing instead on personal empowerment will help you reach a greater state of thriving after abuse. Believing in your ability to change, even before forming the new habit, is a form of thriving in itself. This is because having a positive outlook about yourself is vastly different from the gaslit state of self-doubt that abuse can create.

"Eye On The Prize"

Once you commit, how do you make it more likely you will succeed? The goal in this stage of thriving is to establish self-care as a regular habit. Self-care here is the *prize*. Research conducted by NYU Social Psychologist Emily Balcetis examined the concept of *attentional narrowing* and found that keeping your focus on your target goal makes it immensely more obtainable. In the NYU experiment, which focused on exercise, it was found that participants performed 23% better and felt the physical task was subjectively easier if they focused their gaze on the finish line.

The best way to keep your focus on the finish line of thriving is to block out all the "noise." Self-doubt and criticism, often in the form of negative self-talk, are some common examples of noise that you may be struggling with after leaving an abusive relationship. Kendall Ann

186

was able to block this noise out in favor of positive self-care through meditation, yoga, and sharing her feelings with her therapist as well as friends and family. Once she was able to do these things she started to realized she was ready to make her own choices again and regain her voice. She did this in the grocery store when she finally blocked out her abuser's past desires and instead listened to her own, knowing exactly what she was there to purchase and not asking anyone else's opinion about it. Even bottles of soda can serve as a form of self-care!

With the newfound knowledge about how to commit and the notion that you have the ability to do so, it is time to block out the noise and ask yourself: *How can I possibly fit more joy into my life?* We encourage you to try having a different inner dialogue, something simple and focused. Going forward we offer you this statement:

"I choose self-care."

Remember, once your choice to practice self-care remains consistent and becomes a habit, you eliminate the effort of decision-making. The fewer decisions you have to make in a day, the more energy you have for thriving. Another simple way to reduce unnecessary decision-making in your daily life is through the "capsule" concept. The *capsule wardrobe* is a common example where you have a number of clothing items you can wear interchangeably, but that all create multiple outfit options. As simple as it sounds, it can reduce stress in the morning before you start your day. You can take this concept a step further with capsule meals, where you have specific meals on days where you may encounter more stress. Planning the same breakfast on mornings where you will encounter a stressful commute or high-pressure meeting can help reduce stress and increase thriving.

Once you have chosen self-care in your thriving journey, it can be helpful to take this concept of capsulizing decisions into your self-care routines. Deciding what you would like to do for self-care beforehand makes it more likely you will follow through. It took Kendall Ann a couple of tries to figure out what worked for her. To generate ideas, we have provided a list of pleasant adult activities, inspired by Dialectical Behavioral Therapy (DBT). I often remind my clients that you don't have to carve out a great deal of time and money to engage in self-care. Some of the things on this list are very simple; some are even free.

187

For this *Thriving Exercise*, take a moment and mark any of the following activities you have done before. Next, circle any that you would like to practice regularly during your thriving journey. At the end of the list you will find a few blank entries. Feel free to fill those in with anything of interest to you that you do not find on this list. Practicing the concept of repetition to help form habits, you can label any chosen activity with a day or time that you would like to start the activity, and how regularly you would like to do so.

Pleasant Adult Activities Exercise

1. Soaking in the bathtub
2. Collecting things (coins, shells, etc.)
3. Going on vacation, no matter if it is a day trip or something more extensive
4. Going to a movie in the middle of the week
5. Jogging or walking
6. Listening to music
7. Lying in the sun
8. Reading magazines or newspapers
9. Hobbies (guitar, poetry, writing, etc.)
10. Spending an evening with good friends
11. Meeting new people
12. Mindfully cooking something you enjoy
13. Practicing karate, judo, yoga
14. Remembering the words and deeds of loving people
15. Having quiet evenings
16. Taking care of my plants or gardening outdoors
17. Going swimming
18. Doodling
19. Exercising
20. Saying yes to a party invitation
21. Playing golf
22. Playing a team sport you used to enjoy or would like to try.
23. Flying a kite
24. Having discussions with friends

188

25. Having family get-togethers
26. Riding a motorbike
27. Running a track
28. Going camping
29. Singing around the house
30. Painting your nails
31. Practicing religion (going to church, group praying, etc.)
32. Going to the beach
33. Going skating
34. Painting
35. Doing something spontaneously
36. Doing needlepoint, crewel, etc.
37. Driving
38. Singing with groups
39. Playing musical instruments
40. Doing arts and crafts
41. Making a gift for someone
42. Cooking
43. Going hiking
44. Writing books (poems, articles)
45. Sewing
46. Going out to dinner
47. Sightseeing
48. Early morning coffee and newspaper
49. Watching my children (play)
50. Going to a play or concert
51. Going bike riding
52. Walks in the woods (or at the waterfront)
53. Completing a task
54. Collecting shells
55. Photography
56. Going fishing
57. Playing with animals or your pet
58. Reading fiction
59. Writing diary entries or letters
60. Cleaning
61. Dancing

62. Going on a picnic
63. Meditating
64. Having lunch with a friend
65. Doing crossword puzzles
66. Going to museums
67. Lighting candles
68. Getting a massage
69. Taking a sauna or a steam bath
70. Doing woodworking
71. Sitting in a sidewalk café
72. Doing something new
73. Flower arranging
74. Going for tea
75. _____

Once you choose a number of activities you would like to do, you can set an attainable goal to start doing them. The goal Kendall Ann had to meditate for five-minutes per day is a great example of what is called a **SMART** goal.

Specific
Measurable
Attainable
Relevant
Time Bound

Kendall Ann's goal was specific and measurable. Instead of saying, "I will meditate daily," she chose the number of minutes. It was attainable because she did not make a goal that was too lofty for someone just starting their practice. It was relevant to her main goal of thriving because it helped her feel better and reduce panic attacks. Finally, it was time-bound because she set her goal to be daily and would report back to her therapist about her progress.

Habits are born from small commitments built upon each other. Feeling the sense of accomplishment from following through with a commitment is one of the best ways to build self-esteem and self-worth. A positive self-esteem and heightened self-worth are both things you will experience more as you continue to thrive. So far, this chapter has focused on generating ideas for self-care and understanding how to set goals. We have focused on retraining your focus and forming regular habits. Equipped with the knowledge on how to make lasting change, the next section of this chapter will outline some specific self-care practices that are proven effective for healing and well-being.

Self-Care Practices

"You have to feel it to heal it."
~ Unknown ~

How would you treat yourself if you were a dear friend, your child, or someone else you truly loved? After experiencing a lack of healthy love and support from your abuser, learning how to love and support yourself is essential for healing and thriving. Self-love and re-parenting can be difficult to practice after undergoing the trauma of an abusive relationship. The following is an exploration of practices designed to increase your well-being and resilience while reteaching you how to care for yourself in the way you have always deserved.

191

Meditation

Meditation and other mindfulness skills are some of the most powerful and commonly recommended forms of self-care for dealing with stress. After going through the stress of leaving an abusive relationship, starting a meditation practice where you are meant to "clear your mind" may feel nearly impossible. The notion that meditation is meant to erase the mainframe of your mind from all thought is a misconception.

Kendall Ann's therapist was aware of this misconception as well, as she assured Kendall Ann that clearing the mind was not the ultimate goal of meditation. She recognized how Kendall Ann felt – like her mind her mind was constantly running away from her. Our minds are designed to think; such is their entire purpose. Instead of aiming for the impossible, we encourage you to focus on the idea of practice. Every time you meditate will be different and just like life, nothing will be perfect. To help you establish your individual practice, we would like to offer some simple, efficient ways to integrate meditation into your life, as meditation could be one of the best coping skills you could use to thrive.

"If you do not have just five minutes to mediate, then it means you need twenty."
~ Unknown ~

Benefits of Meditation

Meditation is an ancient practice that has gained scientific notoriety through the use of fMRI and EEG. The benefits are vast and powerful and can directly impact your ability to thrive after leaving an abusive relationship. Here are some of the important benefits of meditation that will aid in your thriving journey.

Meditation can lead to volume changes in areas of the brain that are important during the thriving stage. In 2011, Sarah Lazar and her team at Harvard found that eight weeks of Mindfulness-Based Stress Reduction (MBSR) meditation increased the thickness of the hippocampus, the area of the brain responsible for learning and memory. Ever notice how you become more forgetful when you are under extreme stress? You can thank the hippocampus for the glitch. Mindfulness meditation was also determined to increase mass in the areas of the brain responsible for emotion regulation and self-referential processing. These skills are incredibly important during times of stress because **meditation helps to reduce the activity in areas of the brain associated with stress.**

Neuroimaging conducted after the eight-week meditation program also showed a reduction in the mass of the amygdala, the brain area responsible for fear, anxiety, and our stress response. The neuroimaging evidence was supported by self-reports of the participants who experienced anecdotal benefits from meditation. Prolonged stress from abuse or trauma can have a negative impact on the brain but luckily, science supports using meditation to repair some of the damage.

As noted previously, chronic stress can reduce resiliency and is a precursor to developing PTSD and some of its symptoms. Meditation is consistently shown to help reduce stress and improve overall functioning of the brain. It is proven to enhance growth in the structures of the brain that are necessary for a healthy stress response, improves attention and also offers relief from symptoms of social anxiety. For these reasons, we would highly recommend meditation become part your thriving journey when recovering from an abusive relationship.

Starting Your Practice

Learning how to integrate meditation into an already stressful life can feel overwhelming. It can be helpful to start with small goals and build upon those successes. Below, you will find a series of questions that will help you start and establish your meditation practice.

1. How many minutes per day would I like to commit to meditation? *(Many meditate for anywhere from 5-30 minutes. It helps to start with a smaller goal (think SMART goals from the previous section) and work towards a larger goal after your initial success.)*

2. Where is a good place for my practice to take place? *(This is preferably a quiet place where you can be alone, or with someone else who is committing to mediate with you. Some people who do not have privacy in their home will find a space outside, a breakroom at work or even the solitude of their own car.)*

3. What style of meditation would I like to try? *(There are a number of styles you can try such as; guided meditation, insight meditation, focused-attention meditation, body scan, compassion or loving kind-ness meditation, Vipassana meditation, chakra meditation or mantra meditation to name a few.)*

Quick Tips to Enhance Your Practice

Mentally: One thing that meditation is not, is a method to stop your mind from thinking. As mentioned before, our minds are designed as thinking machines. The only thing to expect out of a meditation is that every single session will be different. Letting go of expectations can allow for a more fulfilling experience.

Physically: It is often recommended to be sitting in an upright position with your knees at least parallel to or below your pelvis. This can be achieved by sitting cross legged on a bolster or pillow and letting your knees relax downwards. This position allows for your spine to naturally elongate. Do not aim for a rigid spine, as that can interfere with the flow of energy in your body similar to slouching. Pay attention to the natural curve of your spine.

Some who meditate will close their eyes. As Kendall Ann mentioned earlier, closing her eyes was difficult for her right after leaving her abuser, as it made her feel vulnerable and unsafe. If you also find yourself having this experience, you can choose not to close your eyes and rather find a soft gaze in front of you, which in Yoga is called a *Drishti* gaze.

If sitting upright without back support (especially on the ground or a bolster) does not suit your body, you can opt to use a number of accommodations. You can use a meditation chair with back support that can be placed directly on the ground, or a regular chair with back support and a firm seat. If you are sitting in a chair, try to sit with your weight evenly distributed on each hip. Plant your feet firmly on the floor and allow your arms to rest with your hands in your lap. Your palms can be facing up towards the sky in a gesture of receiving or you can place your hands flat on your legs, palms facing down for a more grounded experience.

Meditation apps or aids: If you are new to meditation or restarting your journey after leaving an abusive relationship, it can be helpful to use a meditation app for further support and guidance. A few popular platform options for guided meditations are; Insight Timer, Head Space, and Calm. You can find guided meditations offered by Dr. Kelley on her teacher page found at https://insighttimer.com/kelleycounseling.

Yoga

Another research-supported method of selfcare that can offer healing is yoga. Yoga is a highly effective way to care for both your body and mind. It was first developed 5,000 years ago in Northern India and has been evolving ever since. There is much more to Yoga than just the postures (asanas) and the physical fitness that many people attribute to it. In fact, the practice of Yoga was first created as a means to achieve a more deepened meditation practice by helping the practitioner gain better control of their senses, improve concentration and mindfulness, help increase breath control through pranayama (breath work) and achieve moments of bliss. Though Yoga has been practiced for thousands of years, only in the last century, has it become widely used in the Western hemisphere.

Yoga For Trauma

Research has supported the use of Yoga to enhance healing after trauma as it helps to "de-armor" your body. De-armoring is the process of releasing tension and physical blockages that result from emotional or physical trauma, as well as unhealthy thought patterns and different repetitive or negative experiences throughout life. Tension in the body is a method of armoring and self-protection from harm, but it does not serve for long-term health and wellness. When you leave an abusive relationship, the threat of immediate danger is often removed. However, it takes time for the body to comprehend that the immediate threat has been removed and the defense mechanisms once used are no longer needed. What this means is that the body will continue to persist in an armored state even if it is not necessarily healthy to do so. Yoga provides breath practices and stretching of tense muscles, helping to release the tension that is no longer needed for remaining in a fight/flight mode. Yoga has been found to be so effective at treating trauma that entire styles and practice sequences are dedicated to survivors of abuse and trauma.

In 2002, David Emerson and his colleagues at the Trauma Center in Brookline, Massachusetts created Trauma-Sensitive Yoga (TSY). TSY is an evidenced-based, adjunctive treatment for complex trauma and PTSD. A defining feature of TSY is that it offers a sense of control and awareness over one's own body. Participants are encouraged to compassionately focus on internal sensations in the body without judgment. This means that students do not need to master postures in any particular way.

Each individual is given the choice in how to modify postures in a way that feels comfortable to them. For example, if a posture suggested in a sequence is a forward fold and reaching for the toes feels constricting or uncomfortable in any way, the teacher will encourage alternatives. They will offer the *choice not the command* to move into the forward fold while offering modifications or even offering the option to stand tall in mountain pose. It is entirely up to the individual. Teachers will also be sensitive to the environment of the room, such as allowing the trauma survivor to have easy access to the door, as well as refraining from any hands-on physical adjustments that may be found in other Yoga disciplines.

Benefits of Yoga for Survivors of Abuse

A common issue with recovering from an abusive relationship is re-establishing a healthy relationship with your own body. *Proprioception*, the ability to feel one's own body in space, and *interoception*, the ability to feel internal cues from the body such as hunger and thirst, are often disrupted as a result of chronic stress from an abusive relationship. Yoga is highly effective at improving both proprioception and interoception by offering a compassionate approach to reengage with your body after experiencing abuse of any kind.

The breath work (pranayama) performed in yoga has also been proven to increase the body's ability to handle stress. Positive effects of breath work include; regulating blood pressure, reducing inflammation and tension, improving focus and improved quality of sleep. Healthy breathing habits are one of the first grounding skills I teach my clients, as without adequate breath the body struggles to self-regulate. Following are some research-supported breath practices you can use to find immediate relief from stress and improve overall wellness during your thriving journey.

Breath Exercises for Thriving

Your breath is a powerful and pivotal part of the body's ability to thrive. Our body looks to our breath for clues about whether we are safe. Effective breathing habits benefit the brain, helping to activate the areas responsible for emotion regulation and an enhanced sense of peace. Shallow, rapid inhalation, often experienced during a panic attack or times of extreme stress, signal the body that we must become more alert for a potential threat. As you receive less oxygen from shallow breathing, the rate at which your body inhales naturally increases. This is because our inhalation triggers our sympathetic nervous system which reduces the ability for our body to rest and relax and charges the muscles to become more rigid and activated. This can be helpful if you are trying to perform a strenuous task, but not if you are trying to be relaxed or engaged socially.

This rapid breathing style becomes an unhealthy habit and further increases stress, especially if you often find yourself in a fight-flight state from having experienced an abusive relationship. Age can also impact our breath quality. If you look at the breathing rates of a young child, they are long and smooth like rolling waves. As we age it is important to train ourselves with breath work, otherwise our breath becomes much more shallow and abrupt. This change in breathing rates can have a negative impact on not only oxidative stress, but also our metabolism, sleep, chronic pain, our immune system and our general overall sense of well-being.

The *exhale* should be a major focus when working on breathing exercises. Exhaling activates our parasympathetic nervous system (PSN). The PSN is responsible for our "rest and digest" response in the body. Exhaling helps to smooth our muscles, slow down digestion and our heart rate and provides an overall sense of calm and ease. We encourage you to pay special attention to your exhale in the following breathing exercises presented in this chapter.

With breathwork you cannot get too much of a good thing. It is important to practice breath work throughout the day, not just when you are under extreme stress. Waiting until you are having a panic attack or feeling completely overwhelmed is a common mistake many people make when practicing breath work. You can retrain your body to handle stress more effectively by practicing breathing exercises regularly throughout your day. Over time, this practice will change your body's natural response to stress.

Some find it helpful to set a "breath break" alarm on their phones or to put other physical reminders such as sticky notes on their mirrors or refrigerators with the word "Breathe". Eventually you will become more intuitive and feel sensations associated with unhealthy breathing. When your breath becomes shallow or strained, you will be signaled to slow down and focus on a deep inhale and slow exhale.

When practicing the following exercises, it is important to take your time. Be gentle with yourself and do not continue any exercise if it makes you feel panicked or light-headed. It takes time to retrain your body how to breathe properly. Thriving takes time and patience. The following breath skills taught are not considered to be beginner skills. Our hope is to provide the skills we find most effective. For beginners or those with panic disorders, some simpler yet still highly effective breath techniques to explore are:

- Box Breathing
- Abdominal Breathing
- Equal Breathing

Alternate Nostril Breathing

Alternate nostril breathing is an ancient yogic breath control practice. It has been proven to aid in relaxation, reduce anxiety and promote general well-being. Numerous studies have also shown improved cardiovascular function, along with the ability to reduce heart-rate during times of stress. Interestingly, presidential hopeful Hillary Clinton was quoted in 2018 saying that she used this breathing technique to help cope with the stress of her election loss and found it to be beneficial.

How to Perform Alternate Nostril Breathing

Focus on keeping your breath slow, smooth, and continuous. Focusing on your breath will help you to remember where you are in the cycle. You should be able to breathe easily throughout the practice.

Step 1: Sit in a comfortable position with your legs crossed.
Step 2: Place your left hand on your left knee.
Step 3: Lift your right hand up toward your nose.
Step 4: Exhale completely and then use your right thumb to close your right nostril.
Step 5: Inhale through your left nostril and then close the left nostril with your fingers.
Step 6: Open the right nostril and exhale through this side.
Step 7: Inhale through the right nostril and then close this nostril.
Step 8: Open the left nostril and exhale through the left side.

This is one cycle. You can continue for up to five minutes. Always complete the practice by finishing with an exhale on the left side.

Bee's Breath

Bee's breath, otherwise referred to as *Bhramari* is a safe and effective breath practice that has great therapeutic potential. Much like the previous breath exercise, the practice of extending the exhale with bee's breath helps to activate the autonomic nervous system, eliciting a sense of peace and calm. Additionally, this breath practice involves creating a buzzing noise with the throat that can help drown out negative thoughts or feelings, as well as help tone the Vagus nerve. (There is a great deal that can be learned about the therapeutic impact of the Vagus nerve and the entire nervous system. To learn more about this important nerve you can refer to Dr. Stephen Porges' work, specifically his book, *The Pocket Guide to the Polyvagal Theory: The Transformative Power of Feeling Safe).*

How to Perform Bee's Breath

Step 1: Find a comfortable position and close your eyes, or if you do not feel comfortable doing so, find something in front of you to focus your gaze on softly.

Step 2: Take two deep breaths in and out your nose first to orient to your breath and body.

Step 3: When you are ready, inhale filling your belly and your lungs.

Step 4: For the entire length of your exhalation, make a low to medium-pitched humming sound in the throat (much like a bee buzzing).

Step 5: Do this practice for as little as six breaths cycles or as long as feels comfortable to you.

Step 6: Return to natural breath and gently open your eyes.

Potential Variations:

- Plugging your ears gently with your thumbs, leaving the rest of your hand free, to enhance the sound of the vibration
- Plugging your ears with your thumbs and gently covering your eyes with your fingers to help elicit a grounding sensation and cut off outside light

Getting the Most Out of Your Breath Practices

If you are new to breathing exercises, it may feel very different from how you are normally accustomed to breathing. You may get dizzy or lightheaded, this is normal. As you practice more often, you'll be able to go longer without the dizziness. If you do get dizzy, or start to feel a sense of panic, stay seated for a minute while resuming normal breathing.

These breathing skills can be used anywhere and at any time. We encourage you to practice as often as you feel comfortable or inspired to do so.

Massage and Therapeutic Touch

For many who have experienced the trauma of an abusive relationship, massage and therapeutic touch can be a very powerful method of self-care to enhance thriving and wellness. It can be difficult to imagine being touched by someone you do not know. The body's armoring response is strong after experiencing abuse and the tendency to tense, withdraw and retreat can be pervasive and subconscious. This response makes sense as you needed to protect yourself from physical abuse and harm during your relationship.

The issue is that continuing this protective response to human touch can have a long-term negative impact. Reteaching your body to trust and respond positively to human contact and care can be incredibly healing. Many of my clients prefer to work with a massage therapist who is trained in working with victims of abuse, which they should have described as a specialty in their business or professional bios. Others prefer females body workers if they were abused by a male partner. The choice is entirely up to you if and when you feel ready to try this form of self-care.

One immensely healing style of body work that is unique from other forms of massage is called Rosen Method Bodywork. Rosen Method Bodywork is an original form of somatic work that addresses physical tension resulting from past trauma. Its unique form of sensitive touch and verbal communication helps people become aware of what they are holding in their bodies. This heightened awareness can offer a release of emotions connected to areas of tension and pain. Effectively trained Rosen Method Bodyworkers will be knowledgeable about how to help you handle these emotions as they surface and will provide a safe space where you can explore these sensations if you choose.

Whether you would like to try massage, or body work geared towards emotional release, such as Rosen Method Bodywork, it is essential to find someone who elicits a sense of safety and trust. If you feel safe doing so, it can also be helpful to share some of your story with the body work therapist regarding your past relationship and experiences of abuse. Sharing with someone you feel you can trust can help to enhance your sense of safety. The act of opening up alone can start moving your body away from the tense state of armoring and towards healing and thriving.

When Coping is Not Healing

One thing that self-care is not is a *Band-Aid*. A Band-Aid skill is just what it sounds like, it is a skill that covers up distressing emotions as opposed to healing them. Some common examples of these types of skills are; substance abuse, emotional eating, aggression towards others, excessive spending, self-harm and isolation. Substance abuse, specifically drinking alcohol, was a Band-Aid skill that Kendall Ann used to escape her emotional pain when she was recovering from her abusive relationship. It may seem obvious that these types of skills are not necessarily healthy, and it can be odd to refer to them as "skills" but that is what they are. *Band-Aid* skills are highly effective, in the short-term, which is why we subconsciously gravitate towards them in times of extreme stress.

One of the problems with these skills is tolerance. It is common for band-aid skills to lead back to unhealthy behavior. The phrase *"hair of the dog"* is a perfect example. After drinking too much, the brain and body are dehydrated, and blood sugar is dysregulated and out of balance. Sleep also becomes disrupted when going to bed under the influence of alcohol, because it is difficult to remain in a deep restorative state of REM. Having another drink to deal with a hangover or acute stress is pretty effective in making you feel better in the short-term. This however is not a sign of thriving. Instead, it is a form of surviving, which you have already endured. This stage of *Thriving* is about growing, and healing and sometimes that means *getting comfortable with being uncomfortable.*

We want to invite you to identify the Band-Aid skills you used while trying to survive your past relationship that you now want to move past during your *Thriving* journey. It takes great courage to be honest, which is truly the first step towards healing, and we applaud your efforts to explore and learn from the past.

Band-Aid Skills Exercise

What "Band-Aid" Skills did I use to survive in my past relationship?

What "Band-Aid" Skills am I still using?

What are the consequences of these skills?

Why is it important to me to find skills that are more healing?

What support do I feel I need to let go of these behaviors?

Planning for Self-Care

After leaving an abusive relationship it can be challenging to feel vulnerable and open to change. Moving past surviving into a space of thriving can feel both exciting and scary, because there is a lot of unknown. The secret here is that you already did the most difficult part, leaving. Now you can really flex your resiliency muscles by thriving through the next stage of your life. To help you do this, we would like to invite you to create a self-care plan based on the skills we have explored in this chapter.

Self-Care Plan

• The reason self-care is important to my thriving is:

• The activities I choose to commit to doing daily for self- care are:

• The activities I choose to do weekly or monthly for self- care are:

• Support I may need to follow my plan:

• We encourage you to create a ***Self-Care Mantra*** that best describes the attitude you want to have about self-care. (For example, "No feeling is final, and I deserve peace")
My Self-Care Mantra is:

• How often will I check back in to ensure I am following my plan?

What I Know Now

1. It's difficult to get out of survival mode.

People who don't know much about trauma (or haven't experienced it for themselves) cannot grasp how hard it is to switch out of the mindset of just getting through the day and into the idea of making life enjoyable again. After living so long in fear, I couldn't let it go; I still had concerns about my safety and well-being. I was afraid that my abuser would come after me or continue to stalk me even though I had a restraining order against him. Several people told me after I left that now I could focus on being happy again, like the fears and pain had magically disappeared since I was no longer in a relationship with my abuser. This couldn't have been more wrong. Although these well-meaning people were just trying to help, I had to recover from my relationship at my own pace. I had to develop a comfort level with coping and recovery tools. During this time I learned that even a small step toward recovery was a step in the right direction and I should be proud of any positive change I was making. Some days, it was just getting out of bed and making it through the day without bursting into tears if a stranger smiled at me. I learned that it was crucial to be patient with myself.

2. You have to find what works for you.

It was very frustrating when I couldn't find self-care that actually made me feel better. I was even more discouraged when the things I'd used successfully in the past now failed to provide me comfort. I had to remember that I had changed and because of that I needed to find activities that now worked. Every activity did not become my favorite, but at least they kept me busy. Some of the new things I tried are now part of my everyday life! I meditate every day, but I still cannot close my eyes when I do. I've created a meditation corner in my room that helps. I have a soft cushion to sit on and a small wooden table with a backflow incense burner and sparkly lamp. While I meditate, I gaze softly at the smoke rolling through the incense burner and it helps me harness my calm.

You don't know what's going to stick, so try your best to have an open mind. This may feel like the worst time to be vulnerable and try something new, but maybe it's also the best. I tried paddle boarding for the first time after leaving my abuser and the fact that I only fell off the board once gave me a huge sense of pride. I hadn't been proud of myself in years, and this small victory stayed with me for weeks.

3. There is so much power in my breath.

The first time I learned that how you breathe has a powerful impact on your body was during hot yoga. The instructor told us that controlling our breath and breathing slowly would slow our heart rates. Initially, the idea seemed ridiculous to me. How was breath tied to heartrate? Those are two totally different organs! I changed my mind one day when I was in class in a deep knee bend and my muscles were straining. I could feel my heart racing. I took long, slow, controlled breaths and soon felt my heartrate slow. It worked!

Now I use breathwork constantly. I concentrate on how my breath feels when I'm meditating. I control my breathing to lower my heartrate on long runs or after sprints. I use my breath to ground me when I feel an anxiety attack coming on. Harnessing the power of my breath soothes me in situations when I get flustered. It seems so easy and basic, yet it was a skill I had never used before.

What Do You Know Now?

*This section is intended for you to convey your thoughts,
feelings and reflections on what you learned in the chapter by writing
or using other creative forms of expression.*

Chapter 12

Rebuilding Relationships

"Trust in the magic of new beginnings. "

The secrets I had kept from my friends and family felt like lead in my stomach. Even after I told the people I loved most in the world what I'd been hiding, I was still worried about the consequences of keeping those secrets for so long. Would they think I valued my relationship with my abuser over my relationships with them? Would they judge me? Would they trust me anymore?

"You're not a liar," my therapist whispered while handing me a tissue. "You made choices based on someone else's manipulation."

I nodded. "Do you think they're mad at me?" I asked.

My therapist was silent. "Possibly," she finally answered.

That was not the answer I wanted. I wanted her to tell me everything would instantly snap back to the way things were before I met my abuser. I wanted her to say the relationship with my abuser had not affected the other relationships in my life. He had destroyed so many things. It hurt me to know that the relationships I held dear for so long might also be casualties.

"Abuse forces people to keep secrets. It's the nature of abuse," my therapist told me.

I took those words into my heart...and went to work. I sat down with everyone I cared about and told them I was sorry for not telling them the truth about what I had been experiencing and explained why. Everyone I told reacted based on their own experiences and biases.

209

Some found ways to make what happened to me a commentary on my relationship with them. Others revealed their own painful secrets of abuse they'd hidden and were too scared to confess. Overall, I was lucky with how much support and love I received since starting to reveal the truth about my abuse.

Despite how difficult it was to share my story and experiences I somehow found the strength to tell the people I trusted most. Telling my brother was particularly difficult. He responded with pain and anger, "He will never be welcome anywhere I am," he said through clenched teeth. "Don't. Go. Back."

I understood his anger and I could see the fear in his eyes. I was thankful to have his protection after living in terror for such a long time.

Even now, no one except for my abuser and I knows the whole truth. Some details are just too painful to divulge and so they live inside of my heart. Many times, the experiences claw their way into my consciousness and force me to acknowledge their existence. I feel I cannot burden the people who love me most with these memories. These are the secrets I've only told my therapists. Many times, these memories wake me in the middle of the night, covered in sweat. These are the ones that come back when I feel anxious about other things, the last traces of the trauma and fear that once possessed me every hour of the day.

"No one will want you after you tell them the things you let me do to you," my abuser would threaten me. These words echoed in my brain long after I left him, and they made me fearful of dating anyone. How could I bring up the abuse I had suffered? Would I be judged and rejected? Had I changed too much to fall in love again – ever? It was hard to imagine seeing the good in a man when I had seen such evil in another. Maybe the abuse had hardened me and made it impossible for me to appreciate the little moments in relationships that I had once adored. When I thought of dating, I wondered how I was going to explain to someone why I tensed up when they hugged me, or why compliments might make me suspicious about their intent.

"Why don't you like it when I say nice things to you?" a guy I was dating many months after leaving my abuser once asked me. If I had told the truth, it would have been, "Oh, because I know that sometimes when people are nice to you, they are actually full of shit and say the things you want to hear so they can scream at you or strangle you later." Instead I replied, "It's a long story."

The most difficult thing? Learning to trust myself again. To this day I still wonder if I have the tools necessary to choose the right partner, someone who won't manipulate or hurt me. How can I trust that I am capable of choosing properly when I have been so wrong before? How do I know there isn't something inherently wrong with me? How can I be sure I will not choose a man who will abuse me again? These questions still haunt me and I'm not sure I have the best answers to them.

Another thing, I still struggle with is love bombing (or the lack of it) early in relationships. If I am talking to someone I am interested in and they don't seem overly interested in me, I view it as rejection. I think the person is "lazy" and I don't want to pursue anything because their lack of enthusiasm may reflect what they'll be like later in the relationship. I am working on keeping a more rational view of potential partners and not needing to be "love bombed" to make me feel secure.

What I *am* sure of is that I am capable of love and I am worthy of receiving the deep love I desire. I now understand the confusion I felt during my abusive relationship. My instinct was correct. There *was* something deeply wrong with my abuser and his unpredictable behavior. I knew it long before I was ready to admit that I should leave him. My gut instinct was right even though he did his best to mislead me and convince me that his behavior was okay. Now more than ever, I realize my intuition provides all the evidence I need. I can find a good partner and if I run into a bad one, I know I can leave.

Trusting Love Again

After experiencing an abusive relationship it is common to struggle when trying to trust and love again. We attract people based on what we expect and what we have experienced. Knowing how to spot an abuser is a new skill you possess that you might not have previously had. Abusers are masters of disguise who often appear to be higher functioning than they actually are. They tend to create an illusion of positive appearances for the people in your life. The secrecy involved in being in an abusive relationship can create a sense of distance and loneliness for the survivor. For that reason, learning to trust a potential partner again may include opening up about difficult or painful memories. It can feel very exposing to have to explain or justify why you left a relationship. Kendall Ann explored her worry about sharing her past abusive relationship with future potential partners. These strong emotions can trigger emotional flashbacks, a trauma response common after experiencing abuse.

Emotional flashbacks can occur suddenly when you re-experience emotions that were elicited by your abuser such as loneliness, insecurity, or fear. For example, if you are being challenged by someone who displays strong opinions or emotions, you may feel threatened even if that person is not intending to be menacing. Many people call this being "triggered," which is a perfectly appropriate label. An emotional flashback differs from other types of flashbacks for a number of reasons.

Emotional Flashbacks:

- Are not visual in orientation
- Do not have to have a specific memory attached
- Are usually undetectable aside from the accompanying intense feeling of pain, helplessness, fear, confusion, despair, or sorrow
- Are often accompanied by toxic shame due to negative self-talk delivered from the inner critic

The reason emotional flashbacks can arise when trying to love again has a great deal to do with the vulnerability of taking healthy risks. It is important to expose yourself as often as possible to closeness and to healthy people in the midst of a flashback, even though isolating or rejecting closeness may be your first tendency. Being able to work through these flashbacks in the presence of support can increase your sense of self-awareness and safety with others.

Regaining inner confidence and self-esteem are also part of learning to trust and love again. You may need space before finding a new partner, so you can have time to grow and thrive. I often remind my clients that they will meet someone who rises to their current emotional, spiritual, and mental level. If you seek out a relationship when you are feeling your lowest, you may attract someone who "vibrates" at that same low frequency.

To help improve your emotional energy while exploring potential of new relationships, it is also important to give yourself time to grieve. Grieving can release some of the residual low-level energy from your past relationship. One way to do this is by verbalizing how you feel, which can help you ventilate your pain. This is another reason why community and support are necessary. Having someone to listen to you can make a positive difference in your healing and thriving process.

In addition to verbal venting, you can also ventilate emotional pain stored in your body with practices that help release physical tension. One skill you can use to help release tension when you feel a flashback arise is **Systemic Progressive Muscle Relaxation**. This practice helps to relieve tension and to reorient you to the present; it increases mindfulness and reduces the power of flashbacks.

Systemic Progressive Muscle Relaxation

- Start by focusing on your head where your mental energy resides and end by focusing on your toes and the bottoms of your feet. You can move slowly and with great detail, tensing first the eyes, then the jaw, and then the back of the head and so forth
- Tense each group of muscles as you breathe in and count to "5," making sure to tense your muscles vigorously but not to the point of straining
- Hold the group of muscles for up to five seconds as you hold your breath
- Relax your muscles as you breathe out to the count of "5," trying to empty all the breath in your lungs

213

If you would like to receive guidance on how to engage in this practice, Dr. Kelley offers a Progressive Muscle Relaxation audio on her Insight Timer channel.

Time Alone and Dating Yourself

How you spend your time between relationships can be an enriching and healing time. With my clients, I often explore the idea of *dating themselves.* This is when you relearn about your deepest desires and needs and can become fully in relationship with yourself. You will learn to enjoy your own company. Think about the beginning stages of dating someone. You put energy into doing things to get to know and enjoy them. This is what you should be doing with yourself. Some ideas include:

- Asking yourself questions to explore your interests - perhaps journaling about what you discover
- Spending quiet time relaxing in ways that you find most nourishing
- Going out for dinner, watching a movie, getting your favorite coffee, going to the bookstore, indulging in self-care, checking out new music, all without having to consider if someone else wants to be doing any of these things
- Doing new and adventurous things without having to fear that you may be held back by someone else's doubts or criticism
- Learning to trust yourself through doing all of these things, encouraging growth, and regularly forgiving yourself

You are no longer in an abusive relationship; this is a time to get to know who you are without your abuser. By focusing on your own wellness and health, you will be engaging in positive reparenting and self-care. Also, by seeking safety for yourself during this time, you will discover more about the new you. Focusing on your own wants and desires will help get you in tune with the gut instincts that Kendall Ann said she struggled to heed.

One of the best parts of dating yourself (or spending time alone) is that being on your own becomes more comfortable and even enjoyable.

When you become comfortable being on your own, you can listen to yourself more and block out the noise of other's opinions. Being comfortable with yourself makes it **much more difficult for someone to manipulate you.** Negative self-perception creates a weakened relationship with yourself, making you more likely to focus on negative self-talk as opposed to being compassionate. It takes compassion for you to stand up for what you want, need, and deserve. Simply avoiding negative thoughts won't work because the next time you are alone, they will be there to greet you. The only way to reduce negative thoughts is by going *through* them.

For instance, if you tell yourself that you are not worthy of love, you are confirming a negative belief taught to you in your past abusive relationship. To transform this negative self-talk into a more positive state you must meet yourself with compassion and be willing to listen to what you need. When you look to others to provide such needs, you never learn how to depend on yourself. By learning how to enjoy being alone, you are learning how to be completely responsible for your own happiness and well-being. This will make you far less likely to act codependently in future potential relationships or to feel you need to put up with anything less than what you deserve.

Trusting Yourself Again

Doubts and questions in relationships should not be ignored. It is healthy and beneficial to explore these feelings with your partner. You learn a lot about your partner and your relationship by being open with how you feel. This is because the way your partner responds will provide very important information about the emotional health of that person and your relationship. A healthy, securely attached person should be able to provide empathy in response to your concerns. If they do not respond in a supportive manner, or gaslight you by making you feel "crazy" or irrational for your feelings, then your doubts and concerns about that person have been confirmed. You cannot verify a gut instinct without exploring it.

Being open and transparent about difficult feelings can be challenging. Embracing the power of the word "no" is an effective way to explore whether you can trust your relationship with someone. Remember, "no" is a complete sentence and you do not have to explain yourself any further.

215

By being authentic and open early on you can more accurately detect **Red Flags** that might otherwise be missed at the beginning phases of an abusive relationship.

Detecting Narcissism

Reflecting on your past abusive relationship may uncover that you were dealing with a narcissist and their rage. Many who encounter narcissists do not realize the situation they are in until it is too late. This section will offer you specific signs to look for, as well as some of the reasons behind how and why narcissists function as they do. Knowledge is power and can help you eliminate the chance of befriending or getting into a serious relationship with someone who displays these traits.

At its core, **Narcissism** is a sense of elevated and detrimental self-involvement. Psychologists have studied the traits of narcissism and categorized Narcissistic Personality Disorder as:

- An inflated and grandiose sense of self-image
- Having problems with empathy
- Possessing a sense of entitlement
- A need for admiration or attention

Some level of healthy narcissism is normal in the form of self-worth, self-care and self-esteem. This is partly why children are not diagnosed as narcissists, because ego-centrism is a natural trait of childhood. Early on, if a child is given the unconditional positive regard they need, they do not have to turn their functional narcissism into narcissistic rage to get their needs met (which is what some would call "acting out"). If however, the child is not able to maintain a healthy sense of self, whether it is due to emotional neglect or to a lack of safety early on in life, there is a chance the child's self-focus can become detrimental to future healthy relationships. Narcissistic rage takes over people's lives and causes significant problems for both the narcissist and their victims.

There are two distinct types of narcissists, **the grandiose and the vulnerable**. Grandiose types generally seek out positions of power. Vulnerable types can be quiet and reserved while possessing a strong sense of self-entitlement while also being easily threatened or slighted. Looking back at Kendall Ann's relationship it would appear that her abuser may have identified with the vulnerable narcissist category.

Despite these individuals being methodical about appearances, the dark side of narcissism tends to be exposed during long-term relationships. Narcissists are often proficient at keeping positive appearances during the beginning stages of a relationship. Their need for approval and positive feedback outweighs their drive for authenticity and honesty with people they are not intimate with. When their worth or ego is called into question, they can become resentful or hostile. This can lead to dangerous behaviors such as various forms of abuse and intimate partner violence.

Problems caused by these types of psychological abusers are not solely centered on intimate partners; other members of a family unit can also become the target. The arrival of children can be very triggering for these individuals. Psychological abusers generally struggle when children are introduced to any relationship because attention is taken away from them. This is why children often become the targets of abuse, neglect, and scapegoating. *Scapegoating* is when a person is blamed for the wrongdoings or mistakes of others and is another **Red Flag** to watch out for when assessing a new relationship. It sounds similar to *gaslighting* but differs in that it is not always intended to make the scapegoat feel unstable or crazy. Rather the scapegoat serves as a convenient target for blame. The effects that psychological abusers and narcissists can have on children have been explored in depth in other books and articles, and we encourage you to explore the topic further if the experience with your abuser involved children.

Fending Off Potential Narcissists

One of the simplest ways to reduce the chances of getting into serious relationships with a narcissist is to maintain your own **emotional individuation**, which is your willingness to express your opinions when they differ from other's. You can practice this skill in simple ways, such as being open with others about topics like your favorite music or where you would like to go to dinner. When someone struggles to express their own opinions because they feel the need to people please, what they are own opinions because they feel the need to people please, what they are doing is *fawning* and denying their individual self.

Fawning is defined as displaying exaggerated flattery or attention for others. Pete Walker, author of *Complex* PTSD: *From Surviving to Thriving*, examines the connection between the act of fawning and the common traits of codependency. Codependency has been mentioned throughout this book, as it plays a key role in the dynamic necessary for an abuser to sustain control over their victim. Some common behaviors of codependency include:

- Difficulty making decisions in a relationship
- Difficulty identifying your feelings
- Difficulty communicating in a relationship
- Valuing the approval of others more than valuing yourself
- Lacking trust in yourself and having poor self-esteem
- Having fears of abandonment or an obsessive need for approval
- Having an unhealthy dependence on relationships, even to your detriment
- Having an exaggerated sense of responsibility for the actions of others

According to Codependence Anonymous (CODA) there are a number of unique patterns and characteristics of codependency. CoDA's **Patterns and Characteristics of Codependents** may be found at www. coda.org as well as on pages 4 through 8 of *Co-Dependents Anonymous, Third Edition*. Changing these patterns can be difficult, and so finding support through CODA meetings can serve as an excellent resource for recovering from the negative effects of codependency. You can find resources for local and virtual CODA meetings on www.coda.org.

Stopping People Pleasing So You Can Start Thriving

Never apologize for setting boundaries. Part of the journey of trusting and loving again is knowing you have the power to say "no" in any relationship. Boundary setting extends past romantic relationships and applies to friendships, professional relationships, family members, and even interactions with the general public. Practicing "no" as often as possible helps preserve your mental energy to focus on what matters most to you and increases your ability to thrive.

It is not selfish to set boundaries, in fact it can be a form of authenticity and compassion. Establishing healthy boundaries in a relationship allows for both partners to feel comfortable and to establish self-esteem. This begins with setting healthy boundaries at the start of a new relationship concerning who you are (which can be done by spending quality time with yourself as we explored in the previous chapter) and what you want for yourself.

To establish healthy boundaries in the future, it is useful to reflect on what boundaries you did not set in your past abusive relationship. You have the right to identify and voice your needs and expectations going forward. Examples of what healthy and unhealthy boundaries in a romantic relationship look like can be found in the following chart.

Healthy	Unhealthy
Feeling responsible for your own happiness	Feeling incomplete without your partner
Friendships exist outside of the relationship	Relying on your partner for happiness
Open and honest communication	Game playing or manipulation
Respecting differences in your partner	Jealousy
Asking honestly what is wanted	Feeling unable to express what is wanted
Accepting endings	Unable to let go

Courtesy of www.breakthecycle.org

A common theme I encounter with clients in therapy is that many of them proclaim to be "people pleasers." There are a number of negative effects of people pleasing that can impact your ability to thrive such as:

- Emotional Burnout
- Symptoms of Codependency
- Chronic mental and physical health issues due to inflammation from stress
- Lower self-esteem
- A lack of trust in relationships making it difficult to determine whether your relationships are being held together by your own exaggerated efforts to please and appease someone

People pleasing is a symptom of consistently looking to others for your own self-worth. This is why setting boundaries for yourself and what you want and need is exceedingly important when trying to curb the habit of people pleasing. You can still be a supportive, helpful, and kind person while also setting boundaries. Seeking approval from others often drives the desire to people please, however what results is often a lack of respect from the very people you are trying to please. People pleasers commonly draw the attention of bullies. It is less likely that someone of value will want to be in a relationship with a people pleaser because they may perceive their behaviors as weak or concerning.

A common example of people pleasing is excessive apologizing even when there is nothing to be sorry about. Instead of making others feel better, it can often turn people off, making them feel bad for the people pleaser. Some may feel like they have to caretake for the apologizer, which makes a balanced friendship or relationship unlikely.

There are simple ways to curb people pleasing. One simple method is the **90/10 rule**. Focus 90% of your self-worth and appreciation on how you feel about yourself and 10% on how others perceive you. As social beings it is unrealistic to believe we will never care what others think, but the 90/10 ratio encourages a healthy focus on your own feelings. You can check whether you are practicing this rule by using one of the grounding skills explored in the previous chapter (or simply taking a deep breath) to increase mindfulness of your feelings.

Ask yourself whether your choices are made enthusiastically or

220

or because you feel required by others. There are many ways to put yourself first, but this simple question can offer insight that may help reduce further people pleasing. After going through an abusive relationship, it can be hard to shut out negative self-talk and to quiet your inner critic. We encourage you to start where you can. If you feel you can only focus 50/50, start there and work your way up.

Another way to increase your self-worth and reduce people pleasing behaviors is by using compassionate self-talk. By doing so you will increase your belief in your opinions and improve your confidence. Compassionate self-talk has four elements that help make this form of internal communication essential for thriving after abuse and maintaining healthy relationships.

- It uses a kind tone
- Recognizes that your pain, like others, is a universal human experience
- Acknowledges negative emotions without suppressing or exaggerating them
- Acknowledges that you are making the best decision you can based on your situation

The following page has an exercise that comes from one of the leading experts on the topic of self-compassion, Dr. Kristen Neff. This exercise can be used to enhance self-compassion, thus reducing the need to engage in co-dependent or people pleasing behaviors.

221

How Would You Treat a Friend?

You can either think about or journal your response to the following questions.

1. Think about a time when a friend is really struggling and how you would support this person. What kinds of things would you say to them?

2. If you were in the same situation, how would you speak to yourself? How does this differ from what you would say or do for a friend?

3. Additionally, think about things you say to yourself when you are upset with yourself or struggling. Write a list here of the things you have said to yourself in the past or present regarding this issue:

4. Now ask yourself if you would say these same things to a friend.

Getting What You Truly Deserve

After experiencing abuse it can be difficult to trust anyone again, making the beginning stages of a relationship feel uncomfortable. Having a clear vision for what you want in your next relationship can help you feel more in control when choosing who to trust with your heart. As you start thinking about and working on boundaries, it can become easier to listen to your own needs and desires.

You can achieve all these things by practicing *The Law of Attraction.* This philosophy focuses on improving the likelihood of attracting the kind of relationship and person you want in the future. It refers not only to relationships, but also to anything you want to manifest in your life, whether it be a new job, improved health, or other goals and dreams. This law proposes that *similar energies attract each other through thoughts, ideas, people, situations, and circumstances.*

You can put this law into practice by writing down your non-negotiables list, stating exactly what you do and don't want in a potential partner. This is a working, breathing document you can amend whenever you want. It is an excellent way to help organize your wishes, thoughts, and desires. On the following page you will find the Non-Negotiables exercise.

223

Non-Negotiables Exercise

In this exercise we will explore the qualities you would like in a future partner. No desire is too detailed; you deserve everything you can imagine! Once you have written the list, go back through it and underline the "deal breakers," which are traits you absolutely do not want in your future partner or relationships. If someone does not match that specific criterion, challenge yourself to set a boundary before the relationship moves any further. If you are uncertain, you can ask for feedback from a trusted person about this issue.

There is no limit to what you can consider a non-negotiable. In fact you can underline the entire list. If there is not enough room below, feel free to use a journal. Keep a copy of your list somewhere accessible and make it something important on which you regularly focus. It can be helpful to refer to this list when meeting new people, or if you feel the need to reexamine an older relationship.

List all the qualities you would like in a future partner.

1.
2.
3.
4.
5.
6.
7.
8.
9.
10.
11.
12.
13.
14.
15.
16.
17.
18.
19.
20.

What I Know Now

1. Dating myself is fun!

Seriously, I love it! Most Tuesday nights I have a standing date with myself to see a movie in the theater. I buy my favorite candy and sneak it into the theater in my purse (daring, right?) but I buy the largest Diet Coke the theater sells to soothe my conscience. Sometimes, I'll go to dinner before or go out for a fancy martini after (dirty Grey Goose martini with Blue Cheese stuffed olives, if you're wondering). Sometimes I take the time to do full hair and makeup; sometimes I wear yoga pants and a ponytail. Many Sundays I treat myself to my favorite meal – Brunch! Initially I was embarrassed to tell the hostess I was a "party of one," but the feeling eventually transitioned into empowerment. I enjoy my time sipping a mimosa and eating delicious Eggs Benedict, judgment free!

2. I am now a recovering people pleaser.

I have been a people pleaser since I can remember. I used to find it a compliment when people told me I was "easy to please" or how I could be counted on to "go with the flow" but, in fact, the truth is completely different. I was scared to speak up about my own boundaries and needs because I thought I'd be seen as "difficult," which would lead to my being unwanted. I still struggle with this today.

I feel anxiety when my best friend calls me and I'm unable to chat or call back immediately. I'm scared I'll let her down or anger her in some way. That's ridiculous. My best friend and I have a deep emotional bond that won't be ruined because I am too busy to speak with her at the precise time it's convenient for her. Communication should be convenient for both of us! My time and responsibilities are equally as important as hers and she'd never want me to burden myself to please her.

This acknowledgement has been transformative to my life. My needs, desires, and boundaries are just as important as anyone else's and I don't need to sacrifice them to be accepted or worthy of love.

225

3. Are you there, Narcissist? It's me, Kendall Ann.

It appears my propensity to people-please and sometimes be code-pendent are the perfect fit for a narcissist. You're entitled and have an insatiable need for attention and admiration? That's perfect because I will overextend myself in every way to make you happy, so you'll love me! Now that I am working on changing my own behavior in relationships, I'm also able to spot people who have the characteristics of narcissism more quickly. The biggest tell is a lack of empathy. It usually reveals itself when I need to vent about something in my life that is outside of my relationship. A narcissist will demean my feelings and somehow manage to make me feel like their situation is worse than mine. Or they will shrug off my feelings and try to refocus the conversation back to them in some way. In such a case, I keep an eye out for the other signs of narcissism. If they appear, I will not get involved.

What Do You Know Now?

This section is intended for you to convey your thoughts, feelings and reflections on what you learned in the chapter by writing or using other creative forms of expression.

Chapter 13

Happily Ever After?

*"You've always had the power, my dear.
You just had to learn it for yourself."*
~ *Glinda, The Good Witch of the North, The Wizard of Oz* ~

I'd love to say my life kicked into "fairytale mode" after I left my abuser, each day filled with joy and laughter (and possibly even cute, small forest animals helping me with my chores), but that is not the case. There are still challenges for me to overcome because of the abuse I endured, but now I tackle them with a secret weapon, self-acceptance.

PTSD is a sneaky condition. Most of the time it doesn't affect my life in overt ways, but there are times where it takes me out of my body and forces me into a panic. Unexpected, loud noises still cause me to freeze, to sweat, to lose my breath, and to feel like my heart is beating out of my chest. About a year after leaving my abuser I was celebrating a new boyfriend's birthday at a Mexican restaurant with some of his friends. The wait staff surrounded us and sang him a special birthday song punctuated by someone blowing up a brown paper bag and popping it a couple feet behind me. I nearly jumped out of my own skin. Without explanation, I immediately leapt from my chair and ran outside. Panic highjacked my body. I could barely breathe or think, and I struggled to calm down.

Time stood still and I have no idea how long I was sitting on the curb outside the restaurant trying to collect myself. My new boyfriend came out to find me sitting with my head in my hands.

"Um, are you okay?" he asked.

229

People Pleasing Kendall Ann answered, "Oh, I'm fine. I'll be back inside in just one moment."

"Okay," he answered and walked back inside.

I quickly wiped the tears from my face and rose to my feet. Hesitantly, I walked back inside. I could tell by the looks on everyone's faces when I reappeared at the table that I looked like a mess.

"Sorry about that," I whispered and melted into my chair, humiliated.

I managed to make it through the meal without having a total meltdown, but as soon as I set foot into my apartment alone, I crumpled to the floor and cried. My heart was still pounding, and I couldn't keep my hands from trembling. Sensing I was in trouble, Ozzy curled up beside me. I petted him and cried into his fur for hours.

That moment at the restaurant was incredibly difficult, but it is not my entire story. Since then, I've learned many techniques on how to ground myself when a noise causes me to spiral into a panic. More importantly, I've learned that my body's panic reaction deserves no judgment from me. I am not weak or damaged. When I hear a loud noise, my body believes it must protect itself and it prepares for the worst. My body is doing what it was designed to do.

Now that I can handle the response and not be hard on myself about it, it no longer controls me. *This is natural*, I tell myself when panic seizes me. *Do I get upset at any of the other natural functions of my body?* The answer is always "no", and I can use my grounding techniques to regain my composure. Because of this self-compassion, I am no longer afraid to tell those around me when my body goes into panic mode. I experienced this one afternoon when I was having lunch with my boss. A waiter dropped a tray of food behind me resulting in a loud crash.

"Can you please excuse me for one moment?" I asked my boss.

I made my way to an empty room in the restaurant. I could feel my heart racing. I was already sweating, and I was struggling to catch my breath. *This is panic*, I told myself. Then I went through my grounding techniques. I breathed deeply. I made note of the things around me (things I could see, hear, smell, feel). I considered if I was truly in danger or if my body was having a reaction to a stimulus. Within a few moments, I was ready to return to the table.

"I apologize," I said to my boss. "That loud noise startled me and activated a response from my body."

"It really scared me too!" she replied.

Then we continued our lunch and chatted about work related topics. I didn't owe her a justification as to why my body had reacted to the noise, but at the same time I didn't need to deny that anything had occurred. I had rehearsed the narrative with my therapist, so I was ready. I only gave the details I wanted to give. I didn't need to bare my soul to my boss, but I also didn't need to lie or hide out of shame. Through honesty, I have learned to be my authentic self. This is the way my body reacts to loud, unexpected noises and I have learned how to communicate my response to others without feeling secretive or exposed.

Being authentic about my experiences from my abusive relationship has gotten easier over time. Initially I was worried about not being the "perfect" victim. I feared people would blame me and use any flaw I had as an excuse for my abuser's behavior. I have since discovered that most people understand the abuse I endured was because of my abuser's power and control issues and was not a punishment for my misbehavior. Although it was rather easy for others to see this truth, it was difficult for me. My abuser justified and excused his abuse by implying (or outright saying) that I was to blame in some way.

This was yet another one of his lies that I have had to process. Being with loving and caring people who do not blame me for the abuse has helped me on my journey of healing. I accept my imperfections, but I also know that there is nothing I could have done to prevent his actions.

I also accept that I left him when it was right for me. I no longer judge myself for not leaving him as soon as the first **Red Flag** was uncovered, or when the verbal abuse began, or the sexual abuse, or even the physical abuse. I left when I had gathered enough information to decide that the manner in which he treated me outweighed the love I had for him and the hope he would change. I have released myself from the negative self-talk where I took responsibility for his wrongdoings telling myself things such as, "I should have known when he did this or that..." or "I am so dumb for thinking if I did such and such, it would get better." I now realize I made the best decisions I could based on what I knew at the time.

Do I wish I would have left sooner? Yes. But I don't judge myself for staying.

Initially after leaving my relationship, I felt completely lost. I lacked confidence in my ability to make decisions and I didn't trust myself to make even the smallest choice. I was constantly asking others for their opinions on everything I did because I had grown so accustomed to doubting my ability to choose correctly. Now, some years later, I have emerged more confident in my decisions. I know what is not meant for me and I don't ignore or excuse away my feelings or gut instincts about situations. My new confidence has been hard fought, but I trust it to guide the important decisions in my life.

After several years and hundreds of hours of therapy, I thought I'd be able to identify toxic, manipulative, abusive men with ease. But despite all my experience, I still had blind spots.

I fell in love with and married a man who had been my friend for several years. Admittedly, I chose him because he was the exact opposite of my abuser. My husband was well educated, poised, and mild mannered. I was sure he possessed the attributes of a good partner. Unfortunately, I was wrong.

After being so profoundly violated by my abuser, I wanted a partner who was my greatest protector. While we were dating I told my husband the details of my previous relationship and he promised he'd never betray me or allow anyone to hurt me ever again. Unfortunately, this was a promise he routinely broke. My husband consistently violated boundaries I tried to set with him. He purposely withheld important information that impacted our daily lives in order to manipulate and control me.

I found myself constantly struggling to understand why a man who had promised to be a supportive partner would hurt me, particularly when he knew most of the details of the abuse I had endured. Again, I was having to sacrifice my dignity and self-worth to stay in a relationship. The final straw came when he admitted he had secretly incurred a large sum of credit card debt during our marriage. The confession hit me like a ton of bricks. Financial abuse was something I had not faced before, and it was shocking to be the victim of it.

Although the experiences of my past had not inoculated me from choosing the wrong man as a partner, they had taught me that I had the strength to leave a relationship where I was not being treated as a respected equal, so I made the choice to leave the marriage. Getting a divorce is difficult and painful, but it was a necessary step toward leading a complete, happy life not filled with strife and manipulation.

I refuse to see the dissolution of my marriage as a failure. First, even after experiencing abuse by a man I loved, I didn't give up on love entirely and made the choice to love again. I demonstrated the hope and the courage I have always admired in others. Second, I was able to end my marriage when my boundaries were not respected, proof I could remove myself from people and relationships who force me to ignore my own needs to please them. When the relationship no longer brought me peace and happiness I left, providing me a sense of great empowerment.

When I am facing a situation that doesn't feel "right" to me, I take a moment to be really quiet and still. I call it "getting into" my body. I try to listen to whatever my instincts and observations are telling me and then sit with those feelings without being emotionally flooded or (just as bad) pushing them off to the side. I credit this insight to my meditation practice. Before I used meditation, I would become overwhelmed by emotions, making them feel permanent. Now, I take a moment to try to "look" at the emotion or the reaction I am having. I imagine taking the emotion out of my body and holding it in my hands. This makes is easier to process and I don't feel like I'm drowning in what I'm feeling. By doing this, I'm also able to listen to what my gut reactions and instincts are telling me by minimizing the emotional impact of those instincts. I've used this tool in many different areas of my life about everything from whether to resign from a job to transitioning friendships and ending romantic relationships.

I no longer mistrust or cast aside the things that I "know" are right. If someone I am dating comes on too strong and it feels like love bombing, I speak up and look for other signs that could indicate something unhealthy. If someone violates my boundaries, I no longer give them infinite chances to make amends. If a situation feels uncomfortable or feels like it's not serving my best interests, I move on. I understand that I have made miscalculations in my past, but those don't mean all of my ideas, thoughts, and instincts are incorrect.

I now know I am capable of deciding what is best for me without needing someone else to say it's "right." To those who haven't experienced abuse this may seem easy. They don't understand how an abusive environment brainwashes you into believing that your thoughts, feelings, and gut instincts are wrong. This brainwashing is exactly what an abuser wants because it makes it easier to maintain control of you.

I have also learned that to continue gaining perspective, seeking out support is an important part of thriving. My best friend has been an integral part of my journey. She's taught me that when I am in situations where I don't know what I want, I should at least vocalize my feelings and express what I *don't* want. Taking these steps to express myself often helps me feel confident in making choices. Something else I have gained in my journey of thriving is a greater sense of self-acceptance, which has led me to trust when I feel or sense that someone around me is being manipulative. Sometimes it feels like I possess a superpower! When I sense manipulation, I feel it in my stomach. The sensation is more intense now than it was before I met my abuser. It's as if my body remembers what his manipulation felt like and sounds an alarm in my gut when it reappears. I no longer shy away from the feelings; instead, I confront them. My instinct extends to those I care about as well. When I see the people I care about being manipulated by others, I do not hesitate to bring up my observations in a tactful way.

Although my life is not perfect, I am happy. When I was young my mom used to tell my siblings and me, "Life is difficult. When something joyful occurs, you should squeeze out every drop of happy you can!" Because my abuser showed me the darkest depths of fear and desperation, I am now more appreciative of the light, beautiful parts of life.

I now know that thriving looks different for every person who has been abused and every survivor must deal with their abuse in their own way. I needed to turn my pain and fear into something positive. I'm writing this book and I created and host my podcast, *High Heels and Heartache*, in hopes that other survivors will benefit from what I have learned. Most importantly, I want them to know they aren't alone.

I'll never forget the feelings of hopelessness and fear my abuser fostered in me. The sensation of his hands around my neck, the weight of his body pressing my back into the cold, linoleum floor, the weight of his body pressing my back into the cold, linoleum floor, the way his nostrils flared as he screamed at me - these feelings will always stay with me. But these memories are no longer my prison and are rarely called to mind. Instead, I choose to remember how the people that love me supported me when I needed it most. I remember my dad's hand gripping mine during my restraining order hearing, my mom's warm hug when I was at my lowest point, Christine's laughter at my birthday party, and how the low hum of Ozzy's soft snores comforted me as I lay awake at night.

My story could have ended very differently on that kitchen floor that sunny May afternoon. I could be seriously injured, or worse I could be dead. I am thankful to have escaped with only a minor neck injury, and some emotional wounds that I have been working to mend. Not everyone who is abused is as lucky as I have been, and that fact makes me want to live my life the best way I know how.

I choose to be happy. I choose to accept myself, including all of my decisions. I choose to celebrate the little pleasures in life. I choose to feel negative emotions but will not allow them to control me. I choose to laugh loudly and often and never again to allow someone else to dim my light. But most importantly I choose to believe in myself and accept that even though I am not perfect, I am the only one of me, which is a wonderful thing to be.

Trust Your Instincts

One important fact to know about Kendall Ann's story is that it is not over. She may no longer be in imminent danger, as she is no longer in an abusive relationship, but still she is learning. Making mistakes and learning along the way are an integral part of living a full life. Many survivors have been taught by their abuser not to trust their instincts, but we are encouraging you to do just that. Listen to your feelings and know that there is no one perfect way to thrive after abuse. It looks different for everyone.

Because there are no two survivor stories alike, sharing your story with those you trust can help them to understand what you have gone through. In addition to the support you can receive from opening up about your past experiences, sharing your story can help you to process the beliefs and narratives you created as a response to the trauma. Mainly, sharing your story can offer you greater perspective.

One thing that sharing your story does not do is safeguard against further abuse. As Kendal Ann mentioned, even though she shared the story of her past abuse with her ex-husband, he still financially and emotionally abused her. For this reason, it is crucial to remain vigilant to the **Red Flags** and warnings signs we explored in the pages of this book. If your new relationship becomes unhealthy, end it. You will send a clear signal that you are mindful of what you do and do not deserve.

Integrating Your Story

Finding meaning is an important part of thriving after leaving an abusive relationship. The concept of *integration* is one of the primary goals in therapy centered on trauma recovery. *Trauma integration* is a process in which a past trauma becomes part of your ongoing reality but is no longer the center of your life or experience. This shift in perspective is most often accompanied by new coping mechanisms, awareness and resources that did not exist before the trauma occurred. Kendall Ann mentioned how, after leaving her abusive relationship, she possessed a heightened sense for manipulation that she considered to be a superpower. Her past abusive relationship caused her a great deal of pain and anguish, but she was aware that it also brought her the ability to better protect herself and those she loves.

Another way to integrate trauma is by turning a negative experience into positive action. The act of writing this book and producing and sharing her podcast are both excellent examples of how Kendall Ann has chosen to create positive meaning from the horrific experiences her abuser put her through. As a clinician and aforementioned "wounded healer," I have chosen to do the same with my career. After enduring my own traumas, I became increasingly drawn to learning more about treating trauma. Eventually this led me to focus my treatment approach on clients struggling with their own traumatic histories. I find that integrating my past trauma into my life's work has changed my trauma from meaningless pain into something powerful. My traumas fostered an inner passion that drove me to help others out of some of the darkest places towards healthy, integrated lives.

Moving Forward

If you have ever had the pleasure of experiencing a "Midwestern Goodbye" you will know that it can last anywhere from minutes to hours past the initial attempt to leave a social gathering. There is always one more thing to say, one more hug to give, or one more plan to make. When leaving a Midwestern home you may find yourself having some of the best conversation you've had all visit, with your purse slung over your shoulder, warm leftovers in your hand, waiting to turn the handle on the doorknob to make your exit.

It can be difficult to say goodbye with the fear that you may leave something unsaid. That is how it feels ending this book. There are so many more things that could be shared because as we mentioned, every story is so unique. We are confident that with everything you learned, you are more prepared to identify abuse, leave safely, get the support you deserve, care for yourself, and thrive in the process. We are honored that you trusted us to be part of your journey. Often, picking up a book is motivated by the desire or expectation that the book will change you in some way, especially when you are trying to leave an abusive relationship or make other difficult changes in your life. We hope this book did just that for you. We hope you have learned how worthy you are of love, how to ask for what you want and deserve, and how to continue to be there for yourself with loving kindness. We would also like to encourage you to reach out to us if you have any questions that have been left unanswered at www.ameliakelley.com or www.kendallanncombs.com.

Finally we hope that what you read in this book provided you with the knowledge and the power to get out and stay out. To say "no" any time you need to and to say "yes" to self-compassion. There is a simple and powerful form of meditation called "Metta Meditation" that provides practitioners with a warm- hearted feeling. It can be used to send love and compassion to any and all beings, however you must always start with yourself. You cannot give what you do not have. You must receive the light and love first. So in closing, we ask you to take one more deep breath and repeat this phrase, as many times as you need:

May I be happy, May I be healthy, May I be safe, May I live with ease.

What I Know Now

1. "Forgive yourself for not knowing what you didn't know before you learned it." (Maya Angelou)

During my journey to thrive I kept knocking up against the same metaphorical wall: I should have known better. For years, my support system kept telling me the abuse wasn't my fault and although I was able to accept that as the truth, another part of me kept blaming myself for not leaving sooner. "I should have (fill in the blank)" was the thought I kept repeating to myself. This thought was keeping me from thriving. One day a therapist took me into the bathroom in her office and told me to look at myself in the mirror and repeat after her, "I did not leave him when he screamed at me and called me names, but that doesn't mean I wasn't doing the best that I could at that time." This seemed like a foolish exercise, but I did as she said. Then she told me to repeat after her again, "I did not leave him when he forced me to have sex with him, but that doesn't mean I wasn't doing the best I could at the time." Again, I looked in the mirror and repeated. This exercise went on for five minutes. She told me to repeat all of the "I should haves" that I had told her during previous sessions. By the last repetition I was choking back tears. We went back in her office and wrote down all the things she had me repeat. My homework for the week was to look in the mirror and say those sentences to myself every day. Each day the exercise became a little easier and soon I meant what I was saying. I accepted that I left when I did because I was doing the best I knew how to do at the time of the abuse. This self-acceptance has allowed me to love myself again.

2. I was not ready to integrate my trauma into my life immediately and that is okay.

When I initially left my abuser, I didn't even know what the many forms of abuse were that I had endured. Once I was educated on what abuse is, I was able to start healing the trauma I had experienced. As I was healing I kept thinking about what I would tell Kendall Ann that existed before the abuse. What **Red Flags** would I tell her to look out for? What manipulation tactics would I describe to her in hopes she would see through them? That is what lead me to creating my podcast (which is how I met Dr. Kelley) and to write this book. Maybe if I had the resources of my podcast and this book, some of my pain and confusion would have been spared. Integrating trauma in your life might not look like a podcast or a book but finding a way to turn your pain into power can truly lead to thriving after abuse. I promise it will help your healing.

3. Telling your partner about your previous abuse will not stop them from hurting or abusing you.

I was under the incorrect assumption that knowing the pain and trauma I had endured would prevent a partner from inflicting more pain on me in the future. Just as if I knew you had a broken arm I would not purposely make you carry something heavy. Why would I purposely cause you more pain in a vulnerable spot? Now I know I need to keep my eyes open and listen to my gut instincts when it comes to relationships because I am still learning, and my partner might not have the best intentions. Conversely, I believe that people who truly love me will be there for me and help me heal my trauma. When I am with my mom and there is a loud, unexpected noise, all I have to say to her is, "Loud Noise" and she knows I need a minute to get grounded. She doesn't judge me for it or try to talk me out of my experience. She knows what I need is her presence and her silence while I work through my body's natural response. Clearly explain to people what you need from them in your healing journey so those that love you will honor your healing and give you the support you need to thrive.

240

What Do You Know Now?

*This section is intended for you to convey your thoughts,
feelings and reflections on what you learned in the chapter by writing
or using other creative forms of expression.*

Letters From The Authors

From Kendall Ann

Hello Survivor,

Each survivor of abuse and domestic violence has a unique story containing one common theme: someone you loved tried to control you. No matter where you are in your journey, from discovering you are possibly being abused, to being decades removed from your abuse, you were drawn into a dangerous power struggle that you neither anticipated nor desired.

It wasn't until after I left my abusive relationship that other women told me about their own experiences of abuse. Their stories gave me solace in knowing I wasn't alone. I hope my story provides you some comfort and clarity about your own experiences while Dr. Kelley's insights on abuse and recovery have explained the scientific research about those topics.

I have struggled with feeling ashamed of my abuse. Many times, I have felt blamed and judged when I've shared what my abuser did. What I've come to learn is that the people who blame or judge me do so out of ignorance or personal agenda. I don't owe anyone an explanation about any choice I made during my abusive relationship, because I was doing the best I could at the time, and so were you. I once read the following: "Never be ashamed of a scar. It simply means you were stronger than whatever tried to hurt you." I've taken those words to heart and it is my wish that you will too!

I want this book to make you feel seen. Your pain and trauma are real, and they will take time to dissect and recover from, but I know you can do it. I hope you can reignite the spark that makes you shine; I pray you're able to find happiness and live a life filled with joy and laughter. There will be difficult days, but there will be wonderful ones too. Celebrate the victories in your life (no matter how small they seem) and find joy in life's little moments (like feeling the warm sun on your skin). It's easy to feel alone as a result of abuse, but you are not. According to the National Coalition Against Domestic Violence, 10 million men and women are physically abused by an intimate partner every year in America. This is not a burden you must carry alone. There are people and organizations you can turn to for assistance. I urge you to reach out to them for help. Use whatever resources are available that you deem as trustworthy to support you in your recovery.

My most ambitious goal is that this book will inspire you to be kind to yourself during your journey of recovery. It's easy to judge yourself and self-berate about things you could have done differently. But by doing so, you're not being fair to yourself. This is the time to become your own best friend. Refrain from blaming yourself for the actions of your abuser. The only person responsible for those actions is the abuser.

It took me several years to reclaim my "sparkle" after the abuse I survived. I choose every day to find something to be happy about, to work towards, or to feel inspired by. You aren't defined by what your abuser did to you and just like me, your sparkle hasn't been erased.

Shine bright!

With Love,
Kendall Ann

From Dr. Kelley

Dear Survivor,

I am truly humbled by you. To endure any form of abuse and to come out the other side is no small feat. It is said that those who endure abuse have strength that not everyone possesses. Some of these strengths include the ability to be resilient, the ability to be flexible, and the ability to remain calm in the face of crisis. These strengths will not be lost once you leave your abusive relationship. Instead they will be strengths you can integrate and offer to those you love and more importantly, to yourself for the rest of your life.

Please remember, it is not always necessary to be "strong" and it is not always necessary to work against adversity. You deserve for things to get easier, and you deserve to feel at peace. I hope this book has helped you to understand that you get to choose what you want in your future relationships. Just because someone uses manipulation or guilt to sustain their relationship with you (whether to feed their narcissism or because they are destructive and broken) does not mean that you have to stay and help them work on themselves. You get to decide how you want to be treated and who you want to invest your time in.

I hope this book has offered a very clear message that you deserve to be taken care of and that you always have the right to set boundaries. I truly hope you have been inspired to put your needs ahead of others, because without your self-worth, life becomes much more difficult. Putting yourself first is not selfish or unhealthy, especially if you have children or are in a care-taking role for others. Self-care is crucial because as we mentioned, you cannot give what you do not have.

Thriving involves an active effort of self-love and self-parenting. These actions and ways of thinking become easier (and eventually second nature) the more you do them. I hope that the skills we explored in this book remind you of passions you once had before your abusive relationship occurred or provided ideas for potential new ones. You absolutely do not need to call yourself a "writer" to journal about your experiences, a "painter" to put brush to canvas, or a "yogi" to practice yoga. Every effort you make to express yourself is exactly as it should be, a way to reconnect with you. Another way to do this is by tapping into your own beautiful breath every day, it is yours alone and you deserve to pay attention to it. Taking the time to breath is a simple and powerful way to choose yourself and your natural ability to thrive. I hope you choose safety, joy, and your right to be loved every day. Doing so is another way of defying the past abuse you endured.

In my role as a therapist I am honored each and every time someone shares their story with me. I am honored that they trust me and are willing to challenge themselves to open up to someone new, and I am humbled by the strength they show in doing so. I want you to know that I am not the only therapist who feels this way. I believe that there is someone out there who is the right fit to hear your unique story. Sometimes it takes time to find that fit, but once you do it is worth it.

As we mentioned in this book, there are other ways to promote healing and share your story if therapy does not feel like the route you want to take. Reaching out to friends, family, religious leaders, support groups, and even exploring your experience through creative arts are just some of the ways to start exploring your story.

Finally we want to offer you continued support because the thriving journey takes time. As you continue to learn and grow you may find there are other resources and information you want to learn about. You can follow the link www.ameliakelley.com or www.kendallanncombs.com for continued support and further resources. This is a journey, not a closed conversation. Finishing this book is the end of one story, and the beginning of a new one, yours.

Wishing you all the wellness the world can offer!

Dr. Kelley

245

About The Authors

Kendall Ann Combs

Kendall Ann Combs is an activist and advocate for the rights of survivors of domestic violence. A survivor herself, she created and hosts the international hit podcast, *High Heels and Heartache*, where she provides listeners with access to mental health experts, and interviews those with inspirational and extraordinary stories. She has been a featured presenter, speaking about the importance of self-care and resiliency for survivors of abuse, at national events including the annual conference of the National Coalition Against Domestic Violence. Kendall Ann has always had a passion for reading and writing and it was one of her childhood dreams to become a published author. In hopes of encouraging future generations to love reading, Kendall Ann earned her BS in English and a M.Ed in Reading Education and taught middle school for several years. When she's not podcasting, speaking, or writing, you can find Kendall Ann reading, training for half marathons, spending time with her family and friends, hiking, and spoiling her dog.

Dr. Amelia Kelley

Dr. Amelia Kelley is a trauma-informed therapist who has conducted research focusing on adult ADHD as well as resiliency and PTSD. Her specialties include being a; Hypno-therapist, Art therapist, Highly Sensitive Person (HSP) Therapist, EMDR-informed therapist, meditation teacher, as well as a Certified Yoga instructor integrating therapeutic yoga and psychotherapy. She is a presenter and writer in the "science-help" field focusing on Highly Sensitive Persons, trauma, motivation, healthy living, and adult ADHD. She is a guest podcast presenter focusing on women's issues and coping with the trauma of unhealthy relationships, as well as a coach and trainer for SAS's Work/Life Program in Cary, NC and a resident trainer for the North Carolina Art Therapy Institute. Her practice is also currently part of the Traumatic Stress Research Consortium at the Kinsey Institute. When she is not counseling, writing, or researching, she is most often entertaining and hosting friends and family, traveling, reading, making music, hiking or running, and day-dreaming about her next adventure.

Red Flags

Gaslighting (p.25)

Walking on Eggshells (p.118)

Temporary Honeymoon Phase (p.27)

False Promises (p.28)

Jealousy Through Isolation (p.40)

Disconnection From Self (p.41)

Stonewalling (p.59)

Negative Self-Talk (p.60)

Substance Abuse (p.61)

Unstable Boundaries (p.81)

Sexual Coercion (p.81)

Strangulation (p.93)

Hoovering (p.111)

Scapegoating (p.217)

References

Carlton, N. (2016). Fear of the unknown: One fear to rule them all? *Journal of Anxiety Disorders*. Vol, 41, pp 5-21.

Finkelhor, D. & Brown, A. (1985). The traumatic nature of child sexual abuse. *American Journal of Orthopsychiatry*. 55:530-541.

Frankl, V. E. (1984). Man's search for meaning: An introduction to logotherapy. New York: Simon & Schuster.

Levine, A., & Heller, R. (2011). *Attached: The new science of adult attachment and how it can help you find- and keep-love.*

Levine, P. A. (1997). Waking the tiger: Healing trauma : the innate capacity to transform overwhelming experiences. Berkeley, Calif: North Atlantic Books.

Simpson, C. & Porter, G. (1981). Self-mutilation in children and adolescents. *Bulletin of the Menninger Clinic*. 45:428- 438.

Najavits, L. (2002). Seeking safety: a treatment manual for PTSD and substance abuse. New York : Guilford Press.

Van der Kolk, B. The compulsion to repeat the trauma: re- enactment, revictimization, and masochism. *Psychiatric Clinics of North America* 1989;12(2):389-411.

Van der Kolk, B. (2014). The Body Keeps the Score: Brain, Mind, and Body in the Healing of Trauma. New York: Viking.

Walker, P. (2014). *Complex PTSD: From surviving to thriving : a guide and map for recovering from childhood trauma.*

CPSIA information can be obtained
at www.ICGtesting.com
Printed in the USA
FSHW010103040122
87368FS